# It's Not
# the How
# or
# the What
# but
# the Who

Claudio Fernández-Aráoz

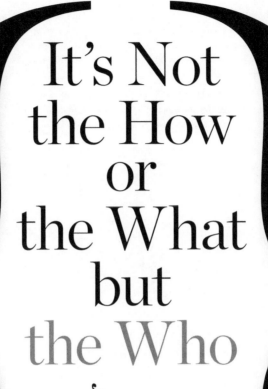

It's Not
the How
or
the What
but
the Who

Succeed by
Surrounding
Yourself with
the Best

HARVARD BUSINESS REVIEW PRESS

Boston, Massachusetts

Library-of-Congress cataloging information forthcoming
ISBN: 978-1-62527-152-5
eISBN: 978-1-62527-153-2

The paper used in this publication meets the requirements of the American National Standard for Permanence of Paper for Publications and Documents in Libraries and Archives Z39.48-1992.

*To María, the love of my life*

# Contents

# Introduction

I'd like to begin with a tale of two CEOs. They have very different backgrounds. They lead very different companies. But they are united by two things: extraordinary leadership success and the relentless focus on talent that helped them achieve it. Both are committed to hiring only the best, to developing their brightest stars, and to uniting them all in exceptional teams—and, as a result, they boost not only their own careers and organizations but also society.

In my twenty-eight years as an executive search consultant, working across all major industries in more than forty countries, I've discovered that the key to outstanding performance and fulfillment—in both work and life—is the ability to surround oneself with outstanding people. This isn't always easy, of course. But these two men have learned how, and my aim with this book is to help you do the same. With the right knowledge, training, and practice, everyone can master the art of great "who" decisions. First, the CEOs' stories.

Jeffrey Preston Jorgenson was born in Albuquerque, New Mexico, in 1964. His mother, the daughter of a US Atomic Energy Commission official, was a teenager at the time; she'd married young and started work as a bank teller in the city, no doubt full of hopes and dreams. Unfortunately, little Jeffrey's childhood started on a sad note: his father left the family not long after he was born. But his mother quickly found love again with a colleague at the bank, Miguel Bezos, a Cuban immigrant who had come to the United States alone at age fifteen, then worked his way through the University of Albuquerque. The two soon married, and Miguel legally adopted Jeffrey, giving the boy his last name.

Little Jeff Bezos showed an early interest in how things worked: He turned his parents' garage into a laboratory, rigged electrical contraptions around the house, and experimented with other projects on the twenty-five-thousand-acre Texas ranch to which his grandfather had retired.[1] As a teenager, he excelled at school, but somehow also found the time to launch his first business, an educational summer camp for fourth-, fifth-, and sixth-graders, which he called the Dream Institute. Fascinated by computers, he went on to study electrical engineering and computer science at Princeton University, then ventured to Wall Street, where he became D.E. Shaw's youngest vice president at age twenty-six.

That's when the idea for Amazon came to him. Bezos had been looking at new ventures in which the company might invest when he came across a startling statistic: the World Wide Web was growing by 2,300 percent *per month*. He drew up a list of twenty potential products he thought might sell well on the internet and quickly settled on books. He quit his job in 1994 and started working out of his own garage with a few software developers.[2]

While most dot-coms launched in the early 1990s went bust, Amazon flourished, with sales jumping from just $500,000 worth of books in 1995 to $61 billion in dozens of product categories by 2012.[3] The company now employs 88,400 full- and part-time workers and, in terms of customer satisfaction, it is consistently rated among the top ten companies in the world, across all sectors. Writing in *Harvard Business Review* in early 2013, Morten T. Hansen, Herminia Ibarra, and Urs Peyer ranked Bezos as the best living CEO in the world (and second only behind the late Steve Jobs) thanks to the $111 billion increase in Amazon's market capitalization up to August 31, 2012, their last day of data collection. And if you think that was due to the good times in the United States and/or the good times for internet companies, think again: Amazon's country-adjusted returns during that period were 12,431 percent, while its industry-adjusted returns were 12,266 percent.[4]

Roger Agnelli was born in 1959 in São Paulo, Brazil. His father, Sebastião, had grown up in the interior of the state, alongside ten brothers and sisters, near the coffee plantation where their own father, an émigré from Italy, had toiled long hours in the hot sun. Although Sebastião had only one day of formal school (he was expelled on his very first day after a teacher broke her finger trying to stop a fight between him and another student), he diligently studied his arithmetic at home with a tutor and eventually found success in adulthood as the inventor of an amazing wood dryer and a top exporter of industrialized wood.[5]

From an early age, Roger loved to visit his father's factory, soaking in its technology, efficiency, and cleanliness. He became passionate about mechanical engineering and planes, but ultimately decided to study economics at the prestigious FAAP in São Paulo. After graduation, he joined the investment banking department of the Bradesco Bank, and eleven years later, at age thirty-three, he was appointed general manager (the bank's youngest ever) of the capital markets unit.

From that perch, Agnelli led more than five hundred IPOs, supporting the local and international development of Brazilian companies, and became deeply involved in the massive privatization of the country's steel, telecommunications, mining, and energy sectors. That's how he came to run Vale. In 2000 Bradesco asked Agnelli to head the administrative council of a privatized mining company in which it had a major share, CVRD (Companhia Vale do Rio Doce, known as Vale). He got to know the people at the company, led a strategy study, and a year later was appointed managing president and CEO. Then, in just one decade, this grandson of a poor immigrant led one of the largest value creations in corporate history.

Agnelli dreamed of the day when Vale would compete with industry giants and, within a decade, he had achieved it. Vale was the largest non-state-owned company in Latin America and one of the twenty largest global corporations. In 2011, the last year of Agnelli's tenure, income was $23 billion on revenues of $59 billion, up from income of $1 billion on less than $4 billion revenue in 2001.[6] Research from The Boston Consulting Group confirms that the company achieved the highest productivity and profitability in the world in the 2000s. Its employment swelled from 11,000 to 190,000, including third parties. It resurrected Brazil's railroad sector and revamped its shipping industry. And it did so while caring for the environment—by, for example, planting or preserving 3 billion trees.[7] The same Hansen, Ibarra and Peyer study ranked Agnelli as the fourth-best CEO in the world, thanks to a $157 billion increase in Vale's market capitalization during his tenure. And if you think that was due to the good times in Brazil and/or the high commodities prices, think again: Vale's country-adjusted shareholder returns were 934 percent, while the industry-adjusted figure was 1,773 percent.[8]

Jeff Bezos and Roger Agnelli have both thrived as CEOs, presiding over monstrous value creation during their tenures. But consider the contrast between their two companies:

- Amazon was a start-up; Vale was an old, formerly state-owned company.

- Amazon was in a hot, new high-tech industry; Vale in a traditional, historic one—mining.

- Amazon was born in the United States, by that time the most competitive, developed nation on earth; Vale is based in Brazil, perceived at the time to be a volatile, high-risk emerging economy.

- Amazon grew organically and mostly in the United States; Vale grew both organically and through M&A and expanded around the world very rapidly.

- Amazon is an extraordinary B2C company delivering incredible customer service and now also sophisticated consumer electronics for personal use; Vale is a classic B2B, a producer of commodity raw materials for industry.

So how did these two men from such different backgrounds lead such dramatically disparate companies to such similar success?

Of course, both are incredible leaders—amazingly bright, hugely ambitious, and strictly disciplined in pursuing their well-crafted strategies.[9] However, in the corporate world—and most other realms of life—no one triumphs on his or her own. Success is rooted in relationships, in the people around you. Bezos and Agnelli recognize this fact, understand it, embrace it. And, in my view, that's the most important trait they have in common. They know that, in order to succeed, *it's not the how or the what but the who.*

In fact, the title of this book paraphrases an answer Bezos gave to an HBR interviewer in 2007.[10] Asked how he'd handled the transition from entrepreneur to manager and leader when so many others fail, he said: "When you start out, it's a one-person thing . . . you're not only figuring out what to do but actually doing it . . . The company gets bigger, and . . . you're mostly figuring out what to do but not how it's done. Eventually you get to the point where you're mostly figuring out who is going to do it, not even what to do. So one way to think about this is as a transition of questions, from "how?" to "what?" to "who?" As things get bigger, I don't think you can operate any other way."

This attitude is evident in Amazon's culture and practices. The company invited me to be a keynote speaker at one of its global recruiting summits in Seattle and to host three workshops for its key senior leaders. This is something I do about a hundred times a year for organizations all over the world, and yet none have people practices that impress me as much as Amazon's. Bezos proclaimed his commitment to getting and developing the best employees and managers in a 1998 letter: "It would be impossible to produce results in an environment as dynamic as the internet without extraordinary people. Working to create a little bit of history isn't supposed to be easy, and, well, we're finding that things are as they're supposed to be! We now have a team of 2,100 smart, hard-working, passionate folks who put customers first. Setting the bar high in our approach to hiring has been, and will continue to be, the single most important element of Amazon.com's success."[11]

From the beginning, Bezos wanted his talent pool to improve with each new addition. And he's stuck to it, reminding colleagues that he'd rather interview fifty people and not hire anyone than hire the wrong person.[12] The key people in his top team have been with Amazon for the last fifteen years, and live and breathe the same core values.[13]

Likewise, Agnelli's extraordinary decade of leadership at Vale stemmed from his decision to surround himself with the best. During a recent meeting, he put it to me unequivocally: "A great team is *the key* for success. The main difference between Vale's practices and those of others was our huge discipline when making senior appointments. We would never hire or promote someone who was not a high performer, highly passionate, and committed to our long-term strategy and demanding objectives." As soon as he stepped in as CEO, he began to work tirelessly with my great colleague Edilson Camara to identify talent, assess development needs, and implement a previously unheard-of meritocracy at Vale: not one senior role would be filled without an objective, independent, professional assessment of all internal candidates and external benchmarks. He hired and promoted some 250 senior executives in this way, all over the world, from the United States to China, Brazil to Mozambique, throughout his tenure. But he says his proudest achievement was the improved quality of the people rising through Vale's ranks, thanks to more effective appraisals, training, and mentoring. "While I always prefer to promote from within, initially I couldn't do it too often because a cultural change was needed," he explains. "After five or six years, though, everyone appointed at the highest levels came from inside."

Bezos continues to lead Amazon and champion the culture, leadership, and people practices that have helped his company thrive. Agnelli left Vale in 2011, following a decade of extraordinary leadership as CEO.[14] Nevertheless, it's clear that both leaders became two of the top four CEOs in the world in the 2000s by making the best "who" decisions they could and then developing their most promising people into stars that shine together. I've focused on their cases because of my personal knowledge of and involvement with the companies, but the CEOs ranked first and third on Hansen, Ibarra and Peyer's list—Apple's Steve Jobs and Samsung's Yun Jong-Yong—by all accounts have the same strategy (see "The Top Four—Putting the 'Who' First" sidebar at the end of this chapter). And I can say the same for every single successful leader I've met in my career, over the course of interviewing some twenty thousand executives, including intimate career conversations with more than four thousand of them. The interactions I've had as a regular guest lecturer at Harvard Business School and a frequent keynote speaker around the world have only confirmed this belief.

Helping people make better choices about their employees, colleagues, team members, project partners, mentors, bosses, friends, and even spouses is the passion of my life because I see how those decisions lead to high-flying careers, happier lives, thriving organizations, and better societies. With this book, I want to help you. I'll start by focusing on the challenges, because there are many—both internal (your unconscious biases) and external (organizational and societal pressures). The first step is to identify the obstacles; the second is to recognize the unprecedented opportunities available if you can overcome them. To that end, later essays will teach you how to identify the best—the people who have the right motives, qualities, and potential to help you excel—with effective assessment tools and strategies. Next, I'll explain how to expertly develop the people you've chosen by encouraging them to become more agile and versatile and putting them together in great teams. Last, I'll show how leaders who do so, like Bezos and Agnelli, not only enrich themselves and their companies but also make the world a much better place for us all.

The essays are grouped as follows:

- Part 1: "The Enemy Within" (recognizing your own failings)

- Part 2: "Outside Obstacles and Opportunities" (understanding external challenges)

- Part 3: "The Right People" (assessing and selecting the best)

- Part 4: "The Bright Future" (helping your stars shine)

- Part 5: "Teams That Thrive" (fostering collective greatness)

- Part 6: "A Better Society" (making great people decisions where they matter the most)

Each chapter might start with a personal story or insights from new academic research but all will end with practical advice on how to master every "who" decision you make and surround yourself with the best—just like Bezos and Agnelli.

## The Top Four—Putting the "Who" First

Apple's Steve Jobs and Samsung's Yun Jong-Yong were ranked first and third in Morten Hansen, Herminia Ibarra, and Urs Peyer's list of top CEO value creators. Not surprisingly, both were also extremely skilled at surrounding themselves with the best:

### Steve Jobs

Steve Jobs, the late and legendary CEO of Apple, had many talents. But according to his biographer, Walter Isaacson, one of his most important leadership lessons was to tolerate only "A" players.[15] As Jobs said himself in 1995, "It is so much more hopeful to think that technology can solve the problems that are more human and more organizational [but] it ain't so. We need to attack these things at the root, which is people and . . . the competition that will attract the best."[16] The same year, he noted, "I always considered [it] part of my job to keep the quality level of people in the organizations I work with very high. That's . . . one of the few things I actually can contribute individually."[17]

Jobs was a pioneer in grasping the vast gap between the best and the rest in his field. (For more on this, see chapter 8.) "The difference between the worst taxicab driver and the best taxicab driver getting you across Manhattan might be two to one: the best one will get you there in 15 minutes, the worst . . . a half an hour . . . The difference between . . . a good software person and a great software person is 50 to one. Therefore, I have found, not just in software, but in everything I've done, it really pays to go after the best people in the world."[18] There's no better example than the English designer Jonathan Ive, Apple's senior vice president of design and the creative mastermind behind the MacBook Pro, iMac, MacBook Air, iPod, iPod Touch, iPhone, iPad and iPad Mini.[19]

The people Jobs hired found him to be an extremely tough but inspirational boss. As he told Isaacson, "I've learned over the years that when you have really great people, you don't have to baby them. By expecting them to do great things, you can get them to do great things."[20] As a result, his biography notes, Apple's top players tended to stick around longer and be more loyal than those at other companies.

Finally, Jobs would never hesitate to get the wrong people off the bus: "It's painful when you have some people who are not the best people in the world and you have to get rid of them; but I found that my job has sometimes exactly been that: to get rid of some people who didn't measure up. And I've always tried to do it in a humane way. But nonetheless it has to be done and it is never fun."[21]

### Yun Jong-Yong

Yun Jong-Yong, the CEO of Samsung from 1996 to 2008, brilliantly transformed the company from a leader in the semiconductor business to a monster global player in consumer electronics by focusing not just on technology and manufacturing excellence but also on the top-notch customer service, innovation, and marketing that only talented people can provide. As he put it to me: "When I looked at resources to run a business, I categorized them in five buckets: technology/skill, capital, information, speed, and people. Except for capital, people are instrumental in developing, changing, and utilizing the other three. This is why people were always on the top of my mind throughout my forty-five-year career at Samsung."

His approach, rather unorthodox in Korea, was three-pronged: selectively recruit seasoned, best-in-class executives from outside; promote diversity in the ranks; and train and develop those employees with the highest potential to be stars.

Yun did not hesitate to hire from outside when needed, even at the highest levels. "Because of my own diverse experience—from semiconductor production to TV product development, procurement to country head of an overseas operation—I realized that people from different backgrounds can bring in new perspectives and opinions that will challenge the existing and sometimes stubborn organization. Executives from best-in-class corporations will bring along those corporate cultures."

Yun led big external recruiting efforts at Samsung to ensure that "the flower" of diversity would "bud and bloom." "An exceptional outsider will never be able to go against the mass, and have an impact," he explains. "Talent acquisition needs to be done massively so there is enough probability to succeed." He also cleverly focused these efforts. For instance, Samsung was the first Korean conglomerate to minimize the importance of academic pedigrees in hiring and promotion decisions. Yun further encouraged his HR department to stop favoring only graduates from Seoul National, Korea, and Yonsei universities (as others still do) and instead focus on finding competent, high-potential people from a broader pool of candidates.

Another push was to capitalize on Korea's great female talent, which most of the country's big companies ignore. He specifically instructed his recruiters to aim for a mix made up of at least 30 percent women not only at the entry level but also for senior executive hires.

Finally, development was one of Yun's big priorities. Under his leadership, Samsung launched impressive training centers where young executives learn both functional and soft skills. The company also has MBA partnerships and a cultural immersion program in which Samsung pays for high-potentials to spend one year in a foreign country, learning the local language and customs.[22]

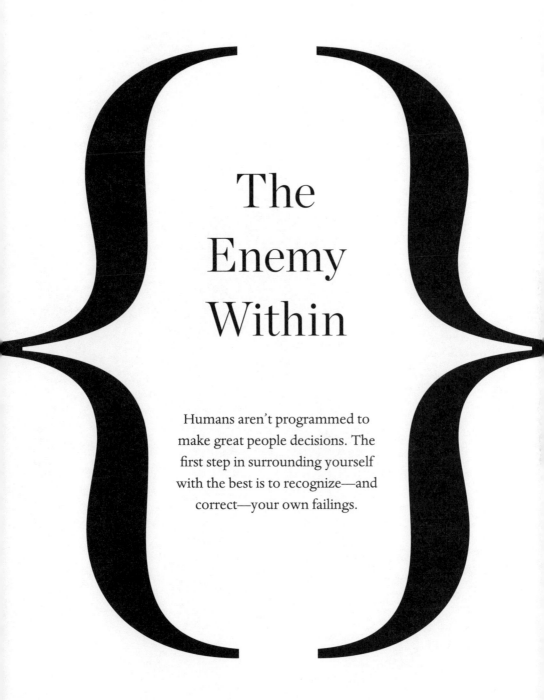

# PART ONE

# The Enemy Within

Humans aren't programmed to make great people decisions. The first step in surrounding yourself with the best is to recognize—and correct—your own failings.

# Prehistoric Hardware;
# Victorian Software

In October 2011, I spoke at the World Business Forum, a gathering of four thousand senior executives and middle managers in New York. I started by asking the audience, "How many of you have made major mistakes while making crucial people choices?" All four thousand people raised their hands.

That group was not alone. All managers struggle to get people right (and if they say they don't, they're lying). As Jack Welch, the legendary former CEO of General Electric, put it to me a few years ago, "Making great people decisions is brutally hard." He confessed that, as a junior manager at GE, he probably got 50 percent of his appointments wrong; thirty years later, as CEO, he was still wrong 20 percent of the time. If it took one of the twentieth century's top corporate leaders three decades to improve his error rate from 50 percent to 20 percent, it's no wonder it's so challenging for the rest of us.

Why are people choices so hard? There are, of course, many reasons; it's difficult to predict your future needs and to quickly and accurately assess traits and skills. I'll address these and other obstacles in later chapters. But first I want to discuss the fundamental problem: we have the wrong brain and the wrong education to get these decisions right.

The human animal is 2 million years old.[1] We have evolved a lot since then, but evolution is very slow, and our brains now are not significantly different than those of the primitive hunters who chased deer in the savanna in prehistoric times. We are therefore thinking, acting, working, deciding on people today with a piece of hardware that is ten thousand years old.[2]

What types of decisions did our primitive ancestor have to make? They involved the four F's: fight, flight, food and . . . well, fornication. The most important question arose when watching something move. It was: "Is that thing going to eat me, or can I eat that thing?" Get it wrong and you might die, either because the deer escaped and you couldn't eat, or because you couldn't escape and the tiger ate you. Those early humans had to do the same with each other. If a stranger arrived at the campfire, how did you decide between fight, flight, or partnering with the person to pursue one of the other F's? You looked for similarities between yourself and the new arrival. If he (or she) looked familiar, you accepted him. If not, you would fight or flee the area. This was an effective strategy then. You're reading this book today because your ancestors, day after day, millions of times, made the right people (and animal) choices. They were the fittest, and they passed their genes—their evolving neural circuitry—on to future generations.

As a result, we humans are still hardwired to make choices in the lower, unconscious parts of our brains—in fractions of seconds, with no deliberation—based on similarity, familiarity, and comfort.[3] We appreciate and trust people similar to us from the moment we're born. For example, a recent study in *Psychological Science* shows that babies prefer not only people similar to them but also people who are mean to dissimilar individuals.[4] And we don't grow out of this tendency. Studies show that adults gravitate toward those with whom they share something, whether it's a common nationality, ethnicity, gender, education, or career path— even the same first-name initial!

As recently as a hundred years ago, when the world was more insular, business less complex, and careers more stable, this primitive, instinctive behavior might not have been such a liability. But today it is a huge one. You cannot be successful in a highly connected, cross-cultural, globally minded environment if you seek support only from others exactly like you. You need to surround yourself with people who have diverse backgrounds and complementary skills, and who properly challenge you.

To make things even worse, our "software" is also obsolete. At the World Business Forum I also asked, "How many of you have studied how to assess people?" Only twenty people—out of the four thousand—raised their hands. That's half of 1 percent! I have asked this question time and again, in some forty different countries, and the response is similar. The vast majority of managers and leaders haven't received the proper education and training on assessing others and helping those around them to reach their highest potential.

As Ken Robinson so powerfully explained it in his 2006 TED talk "How Schools Kill Creativity," our education is dangerously outdated.[5] Kids learn reading and math to a curriculum, but social skills are expected to happen naturally. Even MBA training was born with a major deficit: by 1928, all thirty-four business schools in the United States taught accounting and economics, yet only two taught anything related to what was then called "personnel."[6] That might have made sense at the time, when physical assets and capital were the key production factors, and efficiency paramount. But today, when human capital and innovation determine the future of most companies, it certainly doesn't. And, unfortunately, not much has changed. Erich C. Dierdorff and Robert S. Rubin of DePaul

University conducted a big research study to check the relevance of the typical MBA education by comparing it to an empirically based model of managerial competence (hard evidence about what makes leaders effective) as well as working managers' opinions.[7] The three competencies rated most important in the real world were managing human capital, managing decision-making processes, and managing strategy and innovation. But those three were the least represented in required MBA courses. Only 29 percent of programs offered two or more courses in managing human capital, and a mere 19 percent had two or more focused on managing decision-making processes. By contrast, 87 percent gave that same high weight to managing administrative activities.

We are so lucky to live in a fabulous time, in an extraordinary global village with unprecedented possibilities. You might be reading this on a Kindle, an iPad, or a Samsung tablet, amazing products unthinkable just ten years ago (and developed, I would note, by three of the high-performing, people-master-led companies I talked about in the introduction to this book). While the cutting-edge hardware and software of those devices have optimal functionality for the world we live in, our brains and education systems do not.

The good news is that our neural wiring is much more plastic than we used to believe, and we can teach ourselves to manage it, damping down our primitive instincts and instead tapping into our brain's prefrontal region, or "executive center," to force ourselves into better people decisions.[8] Through disciplined learning and practice Jack Welch became much better at surrounding himself with the best and developing standout leaders. So did Jeff Bezos, Roger Agnelli, Steve Jobs, and Yun Jong-Yong. And you can too—that's the point of this book, after all.

Start by simply acknowledging that you are hardwired for unconscious biases, and that your schools, universities, or organizations haven't worked very hard to change that. It's your job and your opportunity.

# So Sure,
# but So Wrong

For several years, professors at Duke University asked CFOs of large American companies to estimate the return of the S&P index over the twelve months to come.[1] Realizing how hard it is—even for seasoned professionals—to make such a prediction, the researchers also asked the CFOs to offer an "80 percent confidence interval" (that is, the range of returns they would expect with 80 percent probability) as wide as they wanted. By definition, you would expect only 20 percent of surprises. But, when the results came in the following year, a full 67 percent of the actual returns fell out of the CFOs' expected ranges.

We're not talking about amateur individual investors but about some of the world's most successful financial executives. They were quite confident about their estimates, and yet two-thirds of them were wrong. So sure, but so wrong!

Overconfidence in predictions is a pervasive human bias that has a dramatic impact not just on our financial or weather forecasts but also on our people decisions. We all think we're able to accurately judge others even though most of us haven't studied how to do so and, in a business context, typically have fairly limited experience. Those just promoted to a managerial level start from scratch, and even some senior executives lack specific, relevant prior experience. Research my Egon Zehnder colleagues and I conducted showed that some 70 percent of the board members of the largest public companies in the United States and the United Kingdom had never participated in a CEO succession, or had participated in only one. And yet they were the ones responsible for those senior appointments—the most important for any company.

Why are we so sure but so wrong? Because we tend to place too much weight on the information in front of us, without stopping to ask what else we need to know in order to make sound assessments and accurate predictions.

As discussed in chapter 1, our brain is hardwired to make fast people choices based on similarity, familiarity, and comfort. But a more subtle type of bias also comes into play. Princeton economist Daniel Kahneman, who won a Nobel Prize for his work with Amos Tversky on decision making, calls it WYSIATI—"what you see is all there is."[2] Daily faced with an infinite series of inputs and decisions, our minds tend to work mostly on automatic in an effort to preserve energy. This fast, basically unconscious form of thinking (which Kahneman labels *System 1*) is useful a lot of the time. But it also allows us to make up stories out of limited, unreliable, often irrelevant information—and then wholeheartedly believe them— instead of engaging in the conscious, deliberate, analytic thinking (*System 2*) that some decisions (indeed, *all* people decisions) call for. This explains why the CFOs, the board members, and all of us usually feel pretty sure about our views and very rarely consider whether we're wrong.

To illustrate, consider this statement: "Mary graduated with honors from an Ivy League university five years ago and has since worked at an outstanding consumer goods company, where she has been promoted twice." Aren't you immediately attracted by her profile? If you were looking to hire someone in her field, wouldn't you call her right away?

Now consider this statement: "Joe took twice as long as required to graduate and has worked for the last four years for quite an unprofessional family company, from which he was recently fired." What's your immediate impression of Joe? If you were looking to hire someone in his field, would he even make it through your door?

So Mary gets a series of unchallenging interviews and sails through them all. Joe's résumé is meanwhile thrown in the bin. But there are several things I haven't told you about these two candidates. Mary was a C student in college, got her job through a family connection, and is frequently mean and abusive to her colleagues. Joe worked night shifts to pay his way through school and, despite his great contribution and commitment to his previous job, his boss fired him to make room for her own son. In Mary's case, a lack of further inquiry would probably lead you to choose the wrong person. In Joe's case, you'd be likely to prematurely reject a good candidate.

In my experience as an executive search consultant, I see the WYSIATI problem all the time. I have personally handled some five hundred appointments, typically presenting four finalist candidates for each, which adds up to about two thousand people. I attend every interview, carefully watch the interaction between client and candidate, and talk to the client immediately afterward. In the vast majority of cases, the clients focus only on the candidate attributes and experiences that have been explicitly discussed either at the meeting or in the confidential report that I've provided. Very rarely do people ask: "What *else* do we need to know about this person, the role, our company, or our market in order to make a sound hiring or promotion decision?" Unconsciously, we make choices based on what we already know.

In later essays, I'll discuss all the essential elements to check for when assessing people, but for the time being, my advice is simply to become more aware of your overconfident, WYSI-ATI tendencies. The next time you're about to bring someone into your circle—whether it's a team member, business partner, doctor, or nanny—remember that making people judgments is extremely hard and can't be done on automatic. Make a list of what you know and ask yourself what other information you need to make sure you're surrounding yourself with the best. Never miss this step!

{ 3 }

# Inertia

A few years ago, I spoke at a leadership retreat for a leading US life sciences company and asked one group of three hundred executives, "If you were building your organization from the ground up, what percentage of the people would you rehire?" They submitted their responses electronically (and anonymously) and the most common was "about 50 percent." It reminded me of the reply Pope John XXIII gave when a journalist asked him how many people worked at the Vatican. "About half!" he joked.

A few months later, during a workshop for executives at a big equipment manufacturer, I asked the same question of seventeen top leaders. Their confidential answers ranged from 10 percent to 100 percent, but the median answer was 60 percent. That means that, on average, the leaders thought four of ten colleagues were not right for their jobs. When I gave the same quiz to several managers who were participating remotely from seven other locations in Europe, Asia, and Latin America, average answers ranged from 80 percent for those in Switzerland to a dismal 30 percent for their counterparts in one Latin American office.

I ask this question all the time now, and, while the results vary across companies and regions, the fundamental problem is evident: Most of us are bad and slow at getting the wrong people off the bus.[1] As Capital One's CEO Richard Fairbank put it several years ago, "At most companies, people spend 2 percent of their time recruiting and 75 percent managing their recruiting mistakes." It happens in life with poorly chosen friends and romantic partners, as well as at the office.

Whether you made a flawed "who" decision in the first place, you inherited people not of your choosing, circumstances changed, or the people themselves changed, you can't let inertia triumph. If someone isn't panning out, you need to let them know and, often, let them go.

Why is that so hard? Three powerful psychological forces work against us: procrastination, loss aversion, and compassion.

We procrastinate simply because we want to avoid unpleasant things: cleaning out the garden shed, visiting a boring uncle, engaging in tense conversations that involve tough feedback. We don't like to feel uncomfortable. How do you beat procrastination? By making formal commitments. The neuroscientist David Eagleman refers to these as "Ulysses contracts."[2] Just as the mythological hero lashed himself to his ship's mast to make sure he would resist the call of the sirens, you need to prevent your future self from procrastinating on potentially uncomfortable evaluations and decisions. Commit to evaluate each of your team members at regular intervals. Write it down in your calendar, ask your assistant to remind you, and tell your boss you're doing it. In fact, tell your boss you'd like to make those reviews a key personal objective, linked to your bonus.

Our inclination toward inertia is exacerbated by the powerful force of loss aversion. Even if we know we don't have the right people around us, we spend more time worrying about what we might lose than dreaming of what we could possibly gain. For example, most people would reject a bet that offered equal chances of winning $10,000 and losing $10,000. In fact, several experiments have found that the winnings need to be bumped up to at least $20,000—twice as much as the loss—before any significant number of subjects will accept the bet.[3] So, unless the situation is dramatic and the wrong employee becomes a clear and obvious hindrance to others' performance, we prefer to stay with the person we have. We have simply invested too much time, energy, and money, and we aren't willing to gamble that the next hire will be any better. The way to deal with loss aversion is by learning to think like a trader. People who maintain large portfolios of stocks, bonds, or any other assets realize that they're going to win some and lose some. The worst mistake isn't picking a loser but clinging to it as it sinks. It takes discipline to cut your losses and invest your remaining resources elsewhere, but it's as necessary with people as it is with investments.

One more reason for our inertia is compassion. We are all social animals, and most of us find it difficult to create situations that put other people in distress. What about his feelings? His future? His family? As caring and empathetic people, can't we sometimes tolerate less than the best? These are good instincts, but you can put them to work another way—by thinking with compassion not only about the immediate but also the long-term consequences of inaction. If someone significantly underperforms and disappoints you for years and you tell him nothing, what will happen in the end? Your group's performance will suffer, and your resentment (not to mention others') will grow. At some point, you or a subsequent boss will be forced to fire the person at an older age and perhaps in a tougher job market. So you actually increase the chances of a happier ending by offering tough love now. If a colleague isn't meeting your standards, be honest with her; try to help her improve; check whether other jobs and roles could be a better fit. But never stay silent. Candor and concern for those around you are two essential moral obligations of any leader.

In his excellent book *The Outsiders*, William N. Thorndike Jr., discusses the cases of eight individual CEOs whose firms' average returns outperformed the S&P 500 by a factor of 20.[4] Their profiles could not be more different in many ways: one was an astronaut who had orbited the moon, one a widow with no prior business experience, and one was Warren Buffett. But they all had one thing in common: they didn't hesitate to get the wrong people off the bus. Katharine Graham, who found herself at the helm of The Washington Post Company at age forty-six, following her husband's unexpected death, cycled through *four* chief operating officers until she found the right one in Dick Simmons. Only then, finally surrounded by the best, was she able to lead the company into a stunning period of financial outperformance, beating the S&P by eighteenfold and her peers by over sixfold over the next twenty-two years.

Inertia overtakes all of us. In order to beat it, make formal commitments, think like a trader, and compassionately consider long-term consequences.

# Known Devils

Imagine your company is deciding between two finalist candidates for a senior position. One is an insider who's been with the firm for years. The other is an outsider. Knowing nothing more than that, who would you consider to be the safest option? Would your opinion change if I told you the company was highly profitable? What if I told you its recent performance had been subpar?

Years ago, Rakesh Khurana and Nitin Nohria of Harvard Business School conducted a landmark study on the impact that different types of CEO succession had on operating returns in two hundred organizations over a fifteen-year period.[1] They considered four scenarios: (1) an insider promoted in a firm doing well; (2) an insider promoted in a firm doing poorly; (3) an outsider hired to a firm doing well; and (4) an outsider hired to a firm doing poorly. They found that, on average, insiders didn't significantly change their company's performance, which makes sense: similar people working in a similar way in the same company will produce similar results. With outsiders, the result was much more extreme: they added great value, on average, in scenario 4 (when the company was doing poorly) but they destroyed it in scenario 3. Most people conclude from these findings that it's safer to promote from within, particularly if you are doing well. Your answers to the questions I posed at the beginning of this essay probably reflected that sentiment too. But those assumptions ignore the volatility seen in Khurana and Nohria's data.

In their study, the *variance* in results was much larger in *both* the insider scenarios than it was in *both* the outsider scenarios. And the variance was largest in the situation that, on average, seemed the safest: scenario 1, when the company had been doing well and an internal candidate became the CEO.[2] In fact, if you were to calculate a probabilistic range for that scenario—by adding or subtracting two standard deviations from the average effect—the best insider promotions would have multiplied by a factor of *eight* the value of the company, while the worst internal promotions would have destroyed almost 40 percent of its value in just one year![3] When I first saw those findings, I thought there had to be a mistake. How could we possibly expect the largest surprises from familiar candidates? But when I met with Khurana, he confirmed my understanding. Amazing as it sounds, it is indeed riskier to appoint insider CEOs—those "known devils"—than it is to bring in outsiders.

Since then, I've been looking for studies that might make the opposite case but haven't found a single one. I've therefore thought long and hard about the reasons for this "risk of the safe alternative" and discussed it with hundreds of executives and academics. My answer? We simply don't work as hard to evaluate insiders—not only in cases of CEO succession but in all appointments—and this is especially true when things are going well. Our typical approach is to look at likely internal candidates, analyze their performance, and promote the best. We don't worry as much about what the future challenges of the role in question may be, or the critical competencies required to face them. By contrast, when we hire from outside, we're forced to write a proper job spec, consider a larger pool of candidates, grill them in well-structured interviews, and conduct in-depth reference checks. None of this is easy to do with people who are already your colleagues and friends, who will naturally ask, "Aren't my years of contribution and performance sufficient evidence of my qualification? Don't you know me well enough after all this time?"

Don't misunderstand me. I am *not* telling you to always favor outsiders. In fact, I am convinced that the right insiders should be promoted much more frequently than they currently are. In a fascinating piece of emerging research on CEO succession, Gregory L. Nagel and James S. Ang, from Middle Tennessee State University and Florida State University, respectively, have used elaborate multiple regression analyses to estimate what would have happened had companies chosen differently (that is, promoted from within instead of hiring an outsider and vice versa). They concluded that, on average, going outside was economically justified in just 6 percent of the cases, as opposed to the 30 percent of successions in which it's currently seen.[4] Like Khurana and Nohria, they also found that internal promotions created much more value on average, in spite of big variance in the results. Again, the research was on CEOs but, given the dynamics of external recruiting and internal promotions, I think the lessons are applicable to people decisions far down the line. Another advantage to promoting from within is the inspiration it gives to other insiders, which helps keep your talent pipeline strong and motivated. After all, who wants to work for a company where all senior roles are staffed from outside? People need to see they have an opportunity to rise.

In sum, you should always look for opportunities to promote your top internal candidates while also benchmarking against high-quality external ones. Excellent research from the Center for Creative Leadership has consistently shown that the best appointments happen when those hiring consider a wide pool of both insiders and outsiders.[5] Be sure to carefully define the profile of the ideal person, and then invest in a thorough assessment of each candidate. Whether you're shopping for a house or deciding on your next CEO, comparative judgments necessarily produce better evaluations. They are the best way to avoid appointing the wrong outsiders, as well as those known devils who just aren't right for the job.

# The Heat of the Moment

In a candidate, you want to see passion. But as a decision maker, it's something you have to watch, because emotion can seriously impair judgment. If you've ever made a spontaneous purchase you later regretted, there's a good chance it's because the salesperson or the marketing material got you to stop thinking and start feeling: "Sit in the car, take it for a spin. How do you like it?" "Won't your husband love you in that dress?" You were probably also made to feel a sense of urgency: "Let me check whether it's still available." "The sale ends today."

Most of us recognize this—we've all done unwise things in the heat of the moment—but academic research has a funny way of showcasing our human failings in a way that generalities can't. Sheena Iyengar and Raymond Fisman are two Columbia University professors who have investigated the competing roles that passion and logic play in what are arguably the most important people decisions we make—whom to date and marry. One day, after discussing the potential benefits of arranged marriages, they decided to set up a speed-dating experiment to test their ideas.[1] For those of you unfamiliar with today's singles scene, these are events in which several men and women gather in one place and cycle through pairings so each is able to spend a very short time (usually about six minutes) talking one-on-one with every potential mate in the room; once that's happened, everyone writes down who they want to see again, and hopefully some matches are made.

But Iyengar and Fisman added one wrinkle: before and after the event, participants were asked to list what were they looking for in a partner. Consistently (and amazingly), people tweaked their search criteria to more closely match the speed-daters to whom they were most attracted. Those who initially said they were looking for someone intelligent and sincere, yet found themselves drawn to someone attractive and funny, would then decide that was the kind of partner they had wanted all along. However, when the researchers asked participants for their search criteria again six months later, everyone reverted to what they'd first listed. The heat of the moment was gone.

I've seen this happen time and again in initial interviews between our clients and the candidates we present to them. All the prep work we've done—analyzing the need and listing the required and desired attributes—is thrown out the window when some bright and shiny interviewee wows the room (sometimes with experience, know-how, and skills but more frequently with a charismatic personality or even physical beauty). Even if the attractive traits aren't relevant to the job, the candidate jumps to the top of the list, eliminating all others. And often the halo from that first meeting remains, distracting us from a thorough review to check that he or she meets all requirements for success in the new job. We fall in love, and then WYSIATI ("what you see is all there is") comes into play. We make up a nice story and elegantly rationalize our emotional choices.

How do you avoid the dangers of the heat of the moment? First, like those speed-daters, create a checklist of the skills and attributes you and other stakeholders want to see in a candidate before you start the interview process and review it as you meet people. (For more on this, see chapter 16.) If you're tempted to tweak the list, ask yourself: Has the situation changed, or am I being swayed by the people I've seen? Second, consider enlisting the help of a decision adviser, not to help you evaluate people but to serve as a sounding board. Discuss your impressions with someone who knows you well and can guide you toward cool detachment. Third, try to bring perspective into the situation, following the excellent advice in former HBR editor Suzy Welch's *10-10-10: A Fast and Powerful Way to Get Unstuck in Love, at Work, and with Your Family.*[2] Ask yourself, "How will I feel about my decision 10 minutes from now, 10 months from now, and 10 years from now?" Finally, take some time off. People sleep on decisions for a reason. Even the most visceral emotions can fade very rapidly, often within a day or two.

# Decision Fatigue

I recently heard a story about a man in his sixties who had colon cancer and needed surgery. He went into surgery at 7 p.m., but an hour later, the surgeon came out and told the family that, unfortunately and unexpectedly, the situation was beyond hope. His advice was to provide palliative care and wait for the end; not even chemotherapy or radiation could help. After a day of mental anguish, the patient decided to get a second opinion. Another surgeon operated on him, and twelve years later he is alive and happy.

There's a telling detail in that anecdote. As one of my friends, a prominent Buenos Aires urologist, exclaimed when he heard it, "A surgeon can't possibly schedule a procedure like that at night! You're exhausted! You can't think straight!" The patient, a judge, didn't charge the original surgeon with malpractice for that very reason: he recognized the all-too-human problems of decision fatigue—that is, our tendency to make poor choices when our mental energy has already been depleted on other ones.

Judges are, in fact, particularly susceptible to this. When Jonathan Levav at Columbia University reviewed more than a thousand parole decisions by Israeli judges, he found that criminals were much more likely to be granted leniency at the start of the day and right after a scheduled lunch break than at other times. Amazingly, he reported, "You are anywhere between two and six times as likely to be released if you're one of the first three prisoners considered versus the last three prisoners considered."[1]

Social psychologist Roy F. Baumeister has done similar research, first at Case Western Reserve University, then at Florida State University, to investigate the theory (originally espoused by Sigmund Freud) that the self, or ego, depends on mental activities involving the transfer of energy, and we all have a limited amount.[2] He calls this *ego depletion*. In one of his many experiments, Baumeister invited college students who hadn't eaten for three hours into a lab and split them into three groups. Group 1 was given a plate of tempting, freshly baked chocolate chip cookies, which they were told not to eat, and a plate of radishes, which they were encouraged to eat freely. Group 2 was presented with the same two plates of cookies and radishes but was told they could eat whatever they liked. Group 3 was given no food at all. After a long while, the three groups were given some impossible geometric puzzles, which researchers nonetheless described as "simple." In line with Baumeister's expectations, the members of group 1 gave up much earlier than the other two groups. Resisting the cookies had depleted their limited stock of mental energy, and so they threw up their hands in defeat.

Ego depletion explains why nice people get mad at the end of a tough day, why we buy and eat junk food, why the doctor at the beginning of this essay gave such poor advice to his patient, and why judges are tougher later in the afternoon. It also explains why we sometimes make bad people choices. As Baumeister says,

"Good decision making is not a trait of a person, in the sense that it's always there. It's a state that fluctuates."[3]

The more choices we make throughout the day, the harder each one becomes, so we start looking for shortcuts in two different ways: either acting impulsively without careful analysis, like the doctor in his evening surgery, or simply maintaining the status quo and avoiding choice, like the judges in the afternoon parole hearings. This happens everywhere, individually and collectively, to even the brightest of people. I know of a fine professional services firm that recently had its partner elections. Hundreds of brilliant, thoughtful executives from all over the world met in a room to discuss dozens of candidates, presented one after the other. Dossiers had been reviewed and each case was to be discussed for about ten to fifteen minutes. At some point, however, a controversial case came up, generating heated, complex debate for well over an hour. When it was over, the partners were exhausted but they still had to discuss a dozen candidates, and the rules of the election prevented them from taking a break before all were considered. So what do you think happened? Everyone else on the list was approved almost immediately, with no discussion. Partners started clapping the minute the candidates' pictures were projected; years of professional work and careful assessments were ignored.

So what can you do to avoid ego depletion and decision fatigue getting in the way of great people choices?

First, make sure to schedule important interviews at the right time. When I was spending most of my time assessing candidates for client companies, I would always schedule interviews in the early morning or right after lunch. Second, avoid unnecessary or low-priority decisions. Choosing what to eat for breakfast, where to park the car, which laptop to buy, whether to exercise, where to go on vacation, how to invest your money—all of it depletes your mental power. Try to routinize or outsource as much as possible.

Last, take breaks and eat snacks. Great decision makers never schedule endless back-to-back meetings, and they never work hungry. In Baumeister's experiments, something as simple as sugary lemonade mitigated decision fatigue and sometimes completely reversed it. I make it a rule to take breaks every sixty to ninety minutes, and when I'm peckish I reach for a fruit-and-nut bar!

# PART TWO

# Outside Obstacles and Opportunities

External challenges can also prevent you from surrounding yourself with the best. It's important to understand what you're up against— from shrinking talent pools to lying job candidates—and use the situation to your advantage.

# The Other GDP

Back in 2006, I worked with Nitin Nohria, the current dean of Harvard Business School, and my Egon Zehnder colleagues, to complete a big study on talent, gathering detailed data and interviewing CEOs from forty-seven companies with a combined market capitalization of $2 trillion, revenues of over $1 trillion, and more than 3 million employees.[1] Representing all major sectors and geographies, these firms were all successful, with strong reputations and solid people practices. And yet we found alarming signs that all were about to face a massive talent crunch over the following decade, as a result of three factors—globalization, demographics, and pipelines (I've taken to calling them "the other GDP")—that were dovetailing to create a perfect storm. Eight years later, these forces remain in play, and the situation for companies—and individuals—intent on hiring the best is the same, if not worse.

*Globalization* involves companies reaching beyond their home markets—and competing for the people who can help them do it. In our study, we found that these major global companies were expecting to increase their revenues from developing regions by

88 percent in the coming six years. Not only did that happen, but the International Monetary Fund and other groups are currently predicting that some 70 percent of the world's growth will come from emerging markets between now and 2016.[2] At the same time, firms from those areas are themselves branching out globally.[3] I wrote in the introduction about Brazilian's Vale conquering the world, and several of its compatriot companies have similar ambitions, as do firms from India, South Korea, and China. Indeed, the number of Chinese companies in the global *Fortune* 500 has jumped from just eight in 2003 to seventy-three in 2012, thanks in part to non-domestic growth. Globalization is therefore rapidly increasing the number of competitors in each major geographic market—and they're vying for talent as well as customers.

The impact of *demographics* on hiring pools is also staggering. The sweet spot for rising executives is the thirty-five- to forty-four-year-old age bracket. But due to the aging of the baby boomers, the percentage of people in that range is shrinking dramatically. In our 2006 study, we calculated that a projected 30 percent decline in the ranks of young leaders over the coming years, combined with anticipated business growth over the same period, would leave companies with half the people they needed to thrive. While a decade ago, this demographic shift was affecting mostly the United States and Europe, the problem now extends to many more countries. By 2020, many other large economies, including Russia, Canada, South Korea, and even China, will have more people at retirement age than entering the workforce.[4]

The third phenomenon is related and equally powerful, but much less well known: companies are not properly developing their meager *pipelines* of future leaders in the way they need to. Last year, when Harvard Business School's Boris Groysberg conducted his annual survey of executive program participants, the average rating of companies' leadership pipelines was 3.2 out of 5, compared with an average score of 4 for current CEOs and 3.8 for current top management. Equally troubling, no talent management function was rated higher than 3.3, and critical employee development activities, such as job rotations, were as low as 2.6. In other words, few executives think their companies are doing a good job of identifying and developing qualified people.[5] This should alarm all of us. In many companies I've worked with lately, particularly from developed markets, I've found the factor of 2 at work: half of senior leaders will be eligible for retirement within the next two years, and half of them don't have a successor ready or able to take over in a short period of time. As Groysberg puts it, "Companies may not be feeling pain today, but in five or ten years, as people retire or move on, where will the next generation of leaders come from?"[6]

Taken independently, globalization, demographics, and pipelines will each create unprecedented demand for the right talent in the right place over the next decade.[7] The pace of globalization has never been faster; the imbalance between old and young has never been so dramatic; and the survey ratings of development practices are the lowest I've seen in my long executive search and teaching career. Combine them, and you get the toughest war for talent ever.

During a late 2013 webcast for the *Harvard Business Review* audience, I used an online poll to ask the attendees about the relative importance of the other GDP factors on their organizations. Globalization had at least some importance for 95 percent, while a full 100 percent said demographics and pipelines mattered. Two-thirds said dry pipelines were a very important or crucial concern.

How should you confront these challenges?

Recognize that they present an opportunity at both the individual and team or organization level. If you personally have what it takes, make wise career moves, and passionately work to hone your skills, you'll be in high demand. And, as a manager or leader, if you work extremely hard to hire, develop, and retain the best talent, you will be a step ahead of the rest.

To map out your priorities, take a critical look at the people around you. How will your company or industry's inevitable globalization affect it? Are you facing a demographics threat? What is the strength of your leadership bench? Are there looming vacancies you'll need to fill? New types of hires you'll need to tackle a new geographic market, customer segment, technology or strategy? Who are your most strategic players? The most competent? The most critical? Who would competing teams, units, or companies be most likely to go after? How will you keep them instead?

Also—perhaps most importantly—who are your rising stars? Who could take on a bigger or different role? What training will they need to do so? Development is critical, because if everyone tries to solve the other GDP problem by hiring good people away from competitors, we'll create not just a zero-sum game but a negative-sum one since, as I'll later discuss in chapter 20, workers are much less portable than we think. We can't just rotate talent; we have to help all our people achieve their full potential.

The past several years have been dominated by stories of fallout from the global financial crisis of the late 2000s. Labor statistics show persistently high unemployment in many regions, and alarming rates of joblessness among the young. When it comes to critical global talent, however, the noise in the news hides an important signal: globalization, demographics, and poor pipelines will inevitably make great professionals scarcer than ever in coming years. This will become a huge challenge for most, but an extraordinary opportunity for those visionary leaders determined to surround themselves with the best.

# The Best and the Rest

What's the difference between a typical performer and a highly productive one?

Back in the 1990s, I reviewed the research on this issue and was pretty amazed by the findings. For people in simple jobs—manning an assembly line, for example—a "star" worker was about 40 percent more productive than a typical one. The distribution was bell-shaped (what statisticians would call *normal* or *Gaussian*), with a standard deviation of about 20 percent; most people were close to the average and only a few performed well above or well below it. Strikingly, however, I found that the distance between the best and the rest grew exponentially with the complexity of the job. A top life insurance salesperson, for example, was 240 percent more productive than the average one, while standout software developers or consultants outperformed most peers by 1,200 percent.[1]

Those findings, dating back a couple of decades, had already convinced me about the crucial importance of being able to select and develop the best. But I recently ran across another study that really blew my mind. "The Best and the Rest: Revisiting the Norm of Normality of Individual Performance," by Longwood University's Ernest O'Boyle Jr. and Indiana University's Herman Aguinis, included an amazing amount of research across a wide range of professions: five separate studies, 198 samples, and 633,263 people in fields ranging from academic research to entertainment, politics to sports.[2] In virtually all those professions the authors found a huge difference between the best and the rest. They also found that performance was typically not distributed in the bell curve seen in the blue-collar work studies I'd previously reviewed, but rather in a long-tail (what statisticians call *Paretian* or *power-law* distribution). It's a lot like book sales: millions of titles sell few copies a year, while only a handful sell millions of copies. Figure 8-1 shows a contrast between the two distributions.

FIGURE 8-1

**The best and the rest—long-tail rather than bell curve**

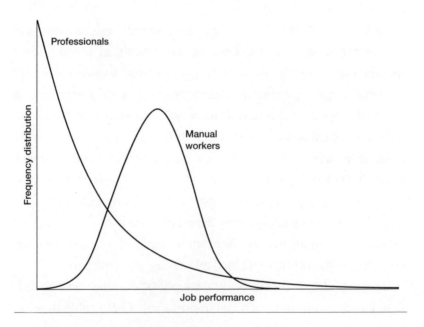

Michael Mankins, Alan Bird, and James Root offer some excellent illustrative contrasts in their *Harvard Business Review* article "Making Star Teams Out of Star Players": the best developer at Apple is nine times as productive as the average software engineer at other technology companies; the best blackjack dealer at Caesars Palace in Las Vegas keeps his table playing at least five times as long as the average dealer on the Strip; the best sales associate at Nordstrom sells at least eight times as much as the average sales associate at other department stores; and the best transplant surgeon at a top-notch medical clinic has a success rate at least six times that of the average transplant surgeon.[3]

The point is that in any profession (but particularly more complex ones) most people have a rather low level of performance, while star performers are very few, yet incredibly valuable. We live in a world where the difference between the best and the rest is huge and growing fast. The author Nassim Nicholas Taleb calls it "Extremistan," and the implications are clear.[4]

It pays to be selective. If you hire "average Joes"—that is, the type of candidate you see most often—you cannot be successful in today's business environment. As O'Boyle and Aguinis concluded, "In an age of hypercompetitiveness, organizations that cannot retain their top performers will struggle to survive."[5] If you instead spend the time and energy to find, develop, and retain stars, you and your company will be leaps and bounds ahead of everyone else.

Also think about your own place in the curve. Average bosses, companies, colleagues, and challenges make you average. Instead, make sure the people above and beside you can help you personally move to the far right of the tail.

# Blissfully Unaware

I often refer to the *typical* interview (not the *right* interview) as "a conversation between two liars." The interviewer (liar 1) starts by painting an unbelievable rosy picture of the company and the job, welcoming the candidate into paradise, and the candidate (liar 2) responds by explaining how great he is, giving the impression that the day he starts work it will be God himself walking in.

Even if the two people are saints who would never consciously embellish their accomplishments or their firms', they are still lying. Here's why: studies have shown that unless you are clinically depressed, your natural tendency is to believe you are much better than you are.[1] Most of us are blissfully unaware about our own abilities and, conveniently, we're all prone to exaggerating our strengths and minimizing our weaknesses. This optimistic bias has its advantages; it boosts self-esteem and helps us execute on what we set up to accomplish. But it makes it difficult for others to accurately evaluate us, and for us to evaluate other people with the same bias, because so much of the information we use—CVs, social media profiles, interviews—is based on self-assessments.[2]

Our degree of ignorance about ourselves in all walks of life is quite amazing. In 1982 two researchers, Paul Mabe and Stephen West, did a comprehensive review of all major studies on self-awareness, observing a very large set of correlations between self-perception and performance. Full awareness translated to a correlation of 1. Yet the average correlation from all studies was only 0.29. In athletics, where feedback tends to be constant, immediate, and objective, the typical correlation was 0.47. However, when it came to business-world studies, the correlation was as low as 0.17 for interpersonal skills, and an incredible 0.04 (basically zero) for managerial competence.[3] This makes sense, of course, because it's much more difficult to assess performance on complex tasks.

In theory, 360-degree reviews should bring us closer to reality, since research has clearly demonstrated that others are usually much better judges of ourselves than we are. Unfortunately, this sort of feedback is often infrequent, threatening, sugarcoated, or too late.

Put yourself in the shoes of someone interviewing for a job, or to join a team. You'll want to put your best foot forward; so you'll both consciously and subconsciously play up your attributes while ignoring your faults. Indeed, psychologists are increasingly finding that it's not just personal traits, such as hubris, that drive our optimistic bias; it's also to a significant extent situational, and some situations actually cause us to be more blissfully ignorant than others. For example, we're more positive when:

- We're assessing ourselves on broad, ill-defined and ambiguous concepts, such as "managerial competence," because we focus on the components or interpretations in which we do better.

- We're taking on new projects or markets because WYSIATI ("what you see is all there is," introduced in chapter 2) makes us ignore the many unknowns.

- We believe we have nothing to lose, which means the unemployed and unhappy are particularly prone to embellishment.

So what can you do to spot this bias toward overconfidence in others and nevertheless surround yourself with the best?

First, carefully check for self-awareness and humility in any candidate. Pat Lencioni, founder and president of The Table Group, points to the two "H's" he looks for in his executives: hunger and humility. Jim Collins found the exact same combination in the "level 5 leaders" that brought their companies from good to great. Does your candidate have both of these things? Can she speak thoughtfully about her weaknesses? Is he driven by personal or social motives?

Second, reduce the social pressure for overly positive self-assessments. When I interview candidates for the first time, I try to focus on the long-term relationship, emphasizing that they should be honest about whether an opportunity is right for them because other, better ones will undoubtedly come along. I tell them that I will check references at the right time, and we agree on a list of people to contact. I never discuss compensation, so the incentive is always on fit, not monetary rewards. All of this will help the candidate be more honest and objective.

Third, give details about what you need, including skills and behaviors, and be as candid as you can about the expected challenges. "Realistic job previews," in which candidates get detailed information about both the positives and negatives of the new job, can help people see themselves in the role. Analyzing forty different studies of this practice, Jean Phillips from Rutgers University has found that it consistently leads to better hires, decreased turnover, and job satisfaction for all sorts of workers: call center employees, grocery baggers, customs inspectors, nurses, army and navy recruits, life-insurance agents, bank tellers, and hotel desk clerks. These previews not only prompt the wrong people to opt out, but they also "vaccinate" your eventual hires to more happily tolerate real life at your company.[4]

Fourth, tell the person to discuss the potential role and his or her readiness for it with close friends and colleagues or trusted acquaintances who are in a similar role or situation—like an impromptu 360. Others know us best, and people are much more open to a candid discussion with members of their own social network.

Finally, make sure to conduct smart reference checks—another big hurdle I'll discuss in chapter 10.

{ 10 }

# Bad Candidate, Great Reference

I've always been an avid reader. In the early years of my career, during my frequent trips from my home in Argentina to the United States, I would spend days perusing books at the best stores, coming home with so many that I often had to buy new bags to fit them. After a while, I decided I couldn't collect any more new luggage, so would start each journey with an empty bag or two to fill. Thankfully, Jeff Bezos launched Amazon.com and changed my life, allowing me to buy any title with the click of a mouse and have it delivered to Buenos Aires within a week. Now I can get my Kindle books within seconds via Whispernet wherever I happen to be, and I don't need extra bags to carry and read them all over the world.

While I have a huge collection, there are a few books I regret not having bought. One that I ran across in the late 1980s was about how to give great references for *bad* candidates. I remember skimming it and laughing at a quote along the lines of "You'll be lucky if you can get this person to work for you," which could mean that the person is a great worker or a very lazy one. But I put the book back on the shelf. For a few years after, I searched for it, but couldn't find it again.

It was twenty years later when I finally did. In January 2012 I was the keynote speaker at the Global Leadership Conference of GMAC, the Graduate Management Admission Council, a non-profit organization of leading business schools which owns and administers the GMAT®. When explaining how hard it is to get reliable references, I referred to the funny little book I had so stupidly passed over. To my surprise, one of the participants raised his hand and shouted: "The author of that book is a good friend of mine, and I'll make sure to get a copy to you!" Sure enough, a few weeks later I received in the mail a dedicated copy of *The Lexicon of Intentionally Ambiguous Recommendations (L.I.A.R.)* by Robert J. Thornton.[1]

It starts with a simple scenario: you work for a big company and a coworker seeking a leadership position at another firm asks you for a letter of recommendation. You've worked with the person long enough to know that, as Thornton puts it, "he can't manage his own sock drawer." Still, you don't feel you can decline his invitation. So what do you do? If you tell the truth in your "recommendation," your colleague won't get the job and you'll have to keep working with him; plus, he might discover that you blocked his opportunity and potentially sue you. If you lie, well, you'll be lying—unless, of course, you follow the artful advice provided in *L.I.A.R.* Chapter 3 includes a list of about 350 intentionally ambiguous sentences and phrases grouped into fifteen or so categories of frequent employee problems, including absenteeism, dishonesty, laziness, lack of ambition, loose morals, and plain stupidity. In case you don't immediately recognize the double meanings, Thornton is kind enough to make them explicit. For example, one suggestion in the absenteeism section is "A man like him is hard to find," meaning either "He's an extremely rare talent" or "We have no idea where he hides." Other phrases I love include "I am pleased to report that he is a former colleague of mine" and the more subtle "I assure you that no person would be better for the job."

Of course, *L.I.A.R.* is a humorous book. But it addresses a serious issue. It's difficult to get completely candid and reliable references on candidates, and thanks to the globalization of business and our increasingly litigious societies, it becomes more complicated every day. Yet you need proper references in order to hire and promote effectively and to surround yourself with the best.

The first reason to check references is that some people, unfortunately, either lie or hide important aspects of their background on résumés and in social media profiles and interviews. I remember a story published in the UK's *Mail on Sunday* about an executive on the board and audit committee of a major British firm. She had claimed degrees she never earned, reported jobs she never held, and changed her name so potential employers wouldn't realize that she'd already served two prison sentences for fraud. In other cases, as I described in chapter 9, people unknowingly overestimate and embellish their attributes while ignoring or downplaying their faults, and it's those lies that references—out of kindness or fear of retaliation—often perpetuate.

Google might sometimes help uncover some blatant deceptions, and routine background checks can help you find more. A recent experimental study by Harvard University's Deepak Malhotra, Lyn M. Van Swol, and Michael T. Braun suggests that other techniques, like watching language, might also work: liars tend to use more expletives, third-person pronouns, and complex sentences than truth-tellers, in addition to being more generally verbose.[2] But you need training to pick up on these things.[3] In my experience, the only way to get close to the whole, unvarnished truth is to have probing conversations with a variety of people who have worked closely with the candidates you're considering.

So, how do you weed out the liars (and the people using *L.I.A.R.* phrases) in the reference process?

First, make sure to agree with the candidate on a comprehensive and relevant list of people to call, including former bosses, peers, and subordinates at several previous places of employment. Narrow your list by thinking about the specific skills you want to measure: former bosses are great at assessing strategic orientation and need for achievement; peers can help to measure influence; subordinates are often the best judges of leadership.

Second, provide the referee with the right incentives. Start the conversation by highlighting how important it is to have a reliable reference, since the candidate in the end won't benefit from getting a job in which he's likely to fail. Explain that you realize no candidate is perfect and all have their individual strengths and weaknesses; plus, it's useful to know as much as possible so if the person is hired you can provide the right kind of integration and support. Emphasize that the referee's comments will be kept completely confidential. And speak in person or on the phone rather than via e-mail; it's easier to solicit the whole truth when you can hear hesitation or emotion in a person's voice or see it on his or her face.

Finally, help the referee avoid frequent biases. Avoid broad questions such as "What can you tell me about Martin?" since the answer would probably focus on his best or most salient general characteristic (rather than the one most relevant to the job), tainting everything that follows since the referee wants to appear consistent. Instead, after checking the person's relationship with the candidate, be specific about the job and its challenges. Ask whether the referee has seen the candidate perform under similar circumstances. And then—only then—ask what the candidate's exact role was, what he did, how he did it, and what the consequences were.

Also study up on those *L.I.A.R.* phrases, so you're able to catch people trying to use them on you!

# The Odds Are
# Against You

We've all heard the stories about the chimpanzees, children, cats, and blindfolded dart throwers who have selected stocks and handily outperformed professional money managers. In the most recent study, researchers from the Cass Business School at City University of London compared 10 million "monkey" indices (that is, ones randomly created and weighted by a computer) to market capitalization weighted indices (that is, the ones investment gurus now recommend over actively managed funds) and found that the monkey funds won every time.[1]

Unfortunately, most people aren't much better than monkeys at people-picking either. If you measure interviewer effectiveness by calculating the correlation between their assessment of a candidate and that person's performance on the job once selected, you get a vast range. Let's say an all-knowing, unbiased, always truthful God has the maximum correlation coefficient of 1.0: he's right 100 percent of the time. Well, the best professional interviewers

(I call them "vice-Gods") stand at about 0.7, and their evaluations are 70 percent accurate. But most people are in the 0.3 range, right only about 30 percent of the time, while the worst professional interviewers give assessments that have a slightly negative correlation (of about –0.1) with performance. If you knew about their incompetence, you would actually do the opposite of what they recommend!

What's more, when it comes to selecting the best, even if you're better than a vice-God, the odds still are against you. I often give people a logic problem to illustrate this point. Imagine that you want to hire only those people whose performance puts them in the top 10 percent of their peer group. Let's also say you're right a whopping 90 percent of the time. That means when you think someone is a top 10 percent performer, you will be right 9 out of 10 times; likewise, when you believe that someone is *not* in the top 10 percent, you will also be right 9 out of 10 times. Now say you're evaluating one hundred candidates over the course of your career. What percentage of the people who you estimate to be top 10 percent will actually be? Stop for a moment to reflect and write down your best guess.

I've done this exercise hundreds of times, all over the world, with thousands of students, professionals, and executives. The responses I typically get from a large crowd usually range from 9 percent to 90 percent. Very few people give the right answer intuitively, and not many more can calculate it.

The answer is 50 percent. You will get it wrong half the time. They say a picture is worth a thousand words; figure 11-1 might help you understand the math.

You start with one hundred candidates. Ten will, by definition, be in the top 10 percent, although you don't know which ones. I've grouped those ten stars at the top of the figure. When you assess those ten, since you are 90 percent accurate, you will rightly consider nine of them to be top 10 percent. However, when you evaluate the other ninety candidates, your 90 percent accuracy will have

FIGURE 11-1

## Odds of picking a top performer (if you're right 90 percent of the time)

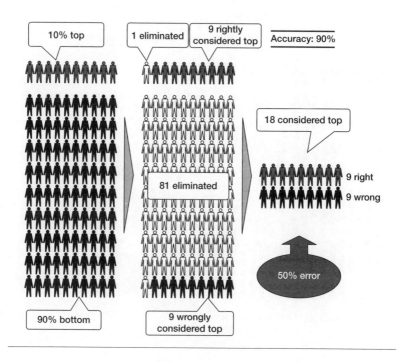

you rightly eliminate eighty-one but wrongly consider nine to be top performers, when in fact they're not. As a result, you'll give a thumbs-up to eighteen players, when only half of them deserve it, and you won't realize the difference between the nine true stars and the nine suboptimal choices.

All of this assumes that you are 90 percent accurate in your assessments, which is impossible for most mortals. If you assume that you are instead 70 percent accurate (now matching the best interviewers as a result of reading this book!), then your error will be almost 80 percent, as in figure 11-2.

However, you can improve your odds with a few best practices.

First, generate a great pool of candidates rather than an average one. Mining companies spend a lot of time and money at the exploration phase, so that they only excavate and refine ore that has a

FIGURE 11-2

## Odds of picking a top performer (if you're right 70 percent of the time)

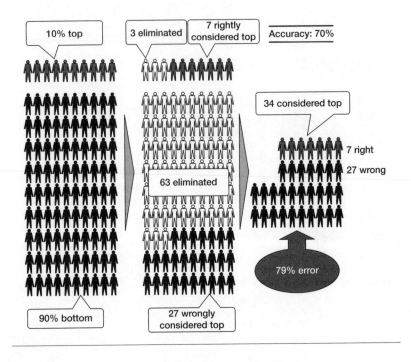

high percentage of the mineral they want. Likewise, you should try to start with a group in which more than 10 percent of people are stars. Find out from relevant sources where the best candidates are and carefully analyze which profiles have worked best for you in the past. When searching for controllers, for example, I have consistently found many great candidates out of the best accounting firms.

Second, try to test people through work samples and practice assignments, rather than using only interviews and reference checking. While this won't be possible for candidates you're considering for complex, high-level positions, there are many standardized jobs in which you can test for competence, from car-part assembly to software coding, from graphic design to speechwriting.

Finally, you should of course ask other people to help you evaluate your candidates. Sequential filters are used in mining to get to the purest gold, and they work in people decisions too. However, as I explain in the next essay, you need to make absolutely sure that you include only a small number of vice-Gods—and no monkeys—in the process.

{ 12 }

# The Problem with Democracy

When executives tell me about the models their organizations use to make people decisions, they often use political metaphors. Sometimes they describe dictatorships, in which team, unit, or company leaders unilaterally decide who is hired, fired, staffed, or promoted. A better version is the benevolent monarchy, in which a king or queen still rules, but ostensibly in the group's best interest. Others say they work in democracies, where all interested parties seem to have a vote or, in extreme cases, veto power. Unfortunately none of those systems works well. What you need is a selective aristocracy—a group of three top-notch assessors per decision to give you valuable input.

I offer this solution not just as an executive search consultant with decades of anecdotal experience but also as an engineer who has taken the time to model its costs and benefits. Revisiting the hypothetical example from chapter 11, let's say you're a vice-God with a 90 percent accuracy rate in predicting top performers. When faced with one hundred candidates, you still get it wrong half the time. But if you involve a second (equally strong) selector, who interviews only the candidates you've approved, she starts off with a higher-quality pool so the chances of a false positive—you both thinking someone is a top performer when he or she isn't—falls to 10 percent. And if you add a third sequential filter, it drops to just 1 percent, as figure 12-1 shows. That's the good news.

The bad news is more filters mean that you're also more likely to eliminate the right candidate for the wrong reasons. You, being 90 percent accurate, will wrongly knock out one top performer, leaving you with nine stars. The second and third interviewers will eliminate two more. With three supercharged vice-Gods, there's already a 27 percent chance of this "false negative" happening (see figure 12-2).

Now imagine what would happen if you required the approval of even more people—adding a fourth, fifth, or tenth filter, as many

FIGURE 12-1

**Three filters eliminate almost all wrong candidates**

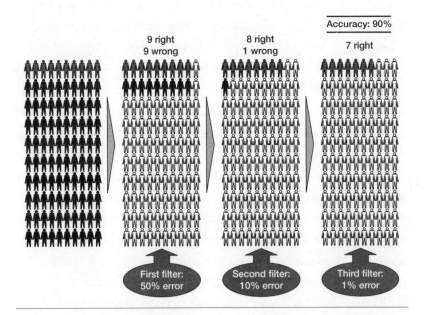

FIGURE 12-2

**However, three filters also eliminate three of ten top candidates**

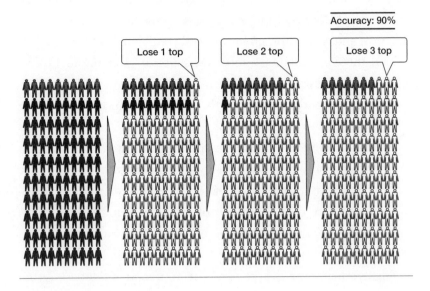

organizations do. Or if you involve the wrong people—those average and worst interviewers I referred to in chapter 11. Bad assessors aren't just monkeys; they're monkeys with machine guns, randomly killing candidates all over the place. And if you let them into your process, it's not a democracy; it's anarchy.

When I explained this to one business school dean a few years ago, he nodded with recognition. "I now see what's wrong with this institution. We give everyone an equal voice and an equal vote, so we very rarely make hiring mistakes—but we've rejected so many candidates who have become star professors somewhere else."

Clearly, hiring or promoting someone destined to be a poor performer is much worse than overlooking a future star. However, given the competition for talent today, any manager who allows great candidates to be arbitrarily eliminated can't win in the long run.

So, how do you form your aristocracy?

First, look for people who truly understand what's needed to succeed in the role and organization for which you're hiring. For purposes of support and accountability, you might want to give priority to the future boss of the new hire (probably you), the boss of the boss, and a relevant, powerful, and credible HR specialist. Aim to have three outstanding interviewers. For me, that number offers a fair trade-off. I'll take a 27 percent chance of bypassing a top performer for a 99 percent chance—the virtual assurance—of avoiding all the wrong ones any day.

Second, choose only people who are motivated to conduct a thorough assessment and make a good decision either because they will benefit from it or because they take great satisfaction in helping others. More than fifty years of research confirms that this is one of the greatest differentiators between great interviewers and terrible ones.[1]

Finally, make sure everyone has been trained in the best assessment techniques, including structured interviews and reference checking. If there isn't time for such training, simply share some of the lessons you've learned in this book. With work, it is possible to turn some of those machine-gun-toting monkeys into vice-Gods.

# Hiring Batting Average

Perhaps you've made a few excellent people decisions in the past and know others who have done the same. But how do you know if you—and they—can repeat that performance? Are you and your fellow assessors really "vice-Gods," who always get people right and can be trusted all the time? Or was your collective success a fluke? Discerning those answers can be challenging. Luckily, the world of baseball offers a solution.

The late Peter Drucker introduced the idea of a *hiring batting average* in the opening paragraph of his classic 1985 *Harvard Business Review* article, "How to Make People Decisions."[1] "Executives make poor promotion and staffing decisions," he wrote. "By all accounts, their batting average is no better than .333. At most, 1/3 of such decisions turn out right; 1/3 are minimally effective; and 1/3 are outright failures." More than two decades later, Jack Welch, the former GE CEO, and his wife Suzy, the former editor of *Harvard Business Review,* coauthors of the book *Winning,* devoted one of their regular *BusinessWeek* columns to the same concept. A reader whose company was expected to double in size over the next year, requiring hundreds of new employees, had e-mailed to ask for some tips on how to hire successfully at such a fast pace.[2]

Naturally, the Welches first emphasized the need to "get religious" about best practices in talent acquisition: ensuring that candidates' values match the organization's, conducting multiple interviews, and carefully checking references. But then they also proposed tracking the HBA, or hiring batting average, of everyone involved in the process to make sure that the top talent-spotters would stay in the rotation, while the worst sat the bench. Each person interviewing a candidate would vote "hire" or "don't hire," with no "maybes" allowed. Six months later, the newly integrated employees would be evaluated by their managers on their performance: below, meets, or exceeds expectations. The company could then calculate the accuracy, or HBA, of each interviewer. If a manager had approved ten candidates and, six months out, eight of them were performing at or above expectations, her HBA would be .800, and she'd get to stay involved in the recruitment push.

This simple technique has at least four great benefits: First, it separates the wheat from the chaff among your interviewers— the "vice-Gods" from the "monkeys with machine guns" who randomly hire or eliminate candidates. Second, it fights inertia, forcing you to review your people decisions early, before the bad ones have time to fester. Third, it prompts interviewers to up their game; as the Welches put it, "If employees know they will ultimately be held accountable for their verdicts—with a hard number, no less—interviews go from chit-chat to real conversation."[3] Finally, it motivates managers to stay in closer contact with new hires, perhaps even to the point of coaching and mentoring them.

TCS, the information systems division of India's Tata, which hires tens of thousands of newly minted college graduates every year, does something similar not with interviewers but with the educational institutions that supply their candidates. The company has calculated the average rate of return for the students hired from each school and, at the schools with the highest HBAs, the company now makes blanket offers to every member of the graduating class. Brilliantly, TCS found a way to be highly selective while spending less time and money in the process.[4]

While of course you won't be hiring hundreds of people, analyzing your personal HBA and that of your colleagues will make you both more effective and more efficient in surrounding yourself with the best. It's a powerful, practical tool to help you hire consistently, with discipline, and to teach others around you to do the same.

Start by measuring your own HBA, and make it a habit. Review all the hiring or promotion decisions you've participated in the past five years, mapping your opinion of the person against their actual performance. Every time you're involved in a new appointment, mark a time six months forward in your calendar to check whether your initial assessment was accurate. You might also check how anyone you recommended for a job elsewhere has done, as well as those candidates you turned down. How frequently do you get your people decisions right? What could you have done differently to increase your HBA?

Then track the HBA of all the people around you, as the Welches recommended, measuring and reviewing it exactly as you do your own. This is particularly important for those colleagues, advisers, and employees you rely upon to help you make your "who" decisions. Plus, there's no better way to encourage their development and career success. The best can only get better if they also learn how to surround themselves with great people.

# Perverse Incentives

Today, in the interior of Borneo, there is a population of a few million Dayak people. They live peacefully now, but in the past, their ancestors were deeply feared for their headhunting practices. The tradition started with rules handed down by a spirit: only those warriors who decapitated their enemies and returned with the heads were able to open the sacred jar used in mourning rituals. But headhunters found many other reasons to pursue the blood sport. Heads were a symbol of power and social status and often used for marriage dowries, as proof that the suitor was brave and capable of protecting his family, community, and land. They were also thought to protect against disease and enemy attack and to promote fertile soil and good harvests. However, the Dayak had very clear guidelines for their headhunting: warriors could not fight a tribe without provocation; surrendering enemies could not be killed; and war leaders were bound to speak only the truth.[1]

Thanks to mass conversions to Christianity and Islam, headhunting in this brutal form has virtually disappeared. But the term lives on to describe my profession. I only wish all executive search firms and consultants had standards as noble as the Dayaks'.

At this stage of the book, you might have thought that it was all a set-up for one recommendation: hire a consultant, like me, to help you hurdle all the internal and external obstacles blocking you from great people decisions. But that's not the only way, or even the best way, to surround yourself with the best. In fact, I believe that the jury is still out regarding the value most search firms add. The best emerging research I've been able to find shows that, at least for large company CEO appointments, their involvement frequently means that highly qualified internal candidates are too frequently ignored, while less-qualified outsiders are too often hired.

Of course, search consultants can add great value in some cases. I remember a backhanded compliment from one Swiss CEO, a long-time Egon Zehnder client, who said, "Listen, Claudio, I don't believe you or your colleagues can properly predict anyone's behavior by assessing them; candidates for senior roles are smarter than you and will always fool you. I work with your firm not for your assessment ability but for your historical knowledge of candidates. You've been following senior executives and observing their performance for years, and that's pure gold."

He's only partially right. Yes, search consultants know many executives well. If you name any two senior managers in Argentina at random, I could probably outline their career histories, explain their ambitions, and tell you what they think about each other. That's because people in our sector tend to specialize in certain geographic markets, functions, sectors, or business situations. However, with all due respect to our Swiss client, many search consultants are indeed better than most at candidate assessment. Given the right training and experience, we learn to identify the critical competencies for each particular role, to drastically improve what we get out of interviews and reference checks, to distinguish potentially great performers from the rest, and to develop deep and trusting relationships not only with candidates but also with sources and references. I would argue that this combination is as valuable as pure platinum.

And yet my profession still probably hurts as much as it helps due to two blatantly perverse incentives: the contingency arrangement and the percentage fee.

Like the original headhunters, most search consultants get power and glory (in the form of compensation) when and if they provide a head. This made sense for the Dayak, when any head would do. But it doesn't work in executive search, when you are looking for the *best* head for a particular job, regardless of who finds it or whether it even needs to be found (as in the case of insiders). Making the fee contingent on the hiring of an outsider brought in by the consultant introduces a perverse incentive to oversell outsiders and shoot down the internal alternatives, even if it's done unconsciously. The solution is to offer a retainer fee, rather than a contingent one, where the search consultant is paid the same no matter who is appointed. That will help him or her objectively assess all possible candidates.

The second perverse incentive is the percentage fee. Traditionally, major search firms are paid a third of the yearly cash compensation (salary plus bonus) of the hired candidate. This again encourages consultants to favor outsiders over insiders, since an organization typically pays a premium of about 30 percent to get an executive to switch companies. The search consultant will also be tempted to present the most expensive, rather than the best, candidates. As a result, the client ends up paying more than necessary. The solution here is to pay a prearranged fixed fee based on the importance of the position and the complexity of the search, rather than a percentage based on the final compensation of the hired candidate.

Even if you have those two things right, you should still use search consultants only in special situations—for example, if your internal candidates are unsuitable or your company is entering a new business, region, or period of strategic change. Then approach the selection of your search consultant as you would any other people decision: consider multiple firms and people, conduct in-depth assessments, and check references. Start by asking relevant colleagues which consultants have consistently delivered strong candidates to them. Once you've developed a short list, meet these consultants in person to check their relevant experience with similar searches, as well as their level of professionalism, candor, and concern. Do you trust them? Will the internal and external candidates trust them? Are they persuasive and inspirational? Also ask how much of the process they delegate to junior staff, making sure that nothing sensitive, such as sourcing or candidate assessment, is. Check the internal collaboration at their firms to see whether you'll have access to their entire collective capital. Only under these conditions will the right search consultants add great value.

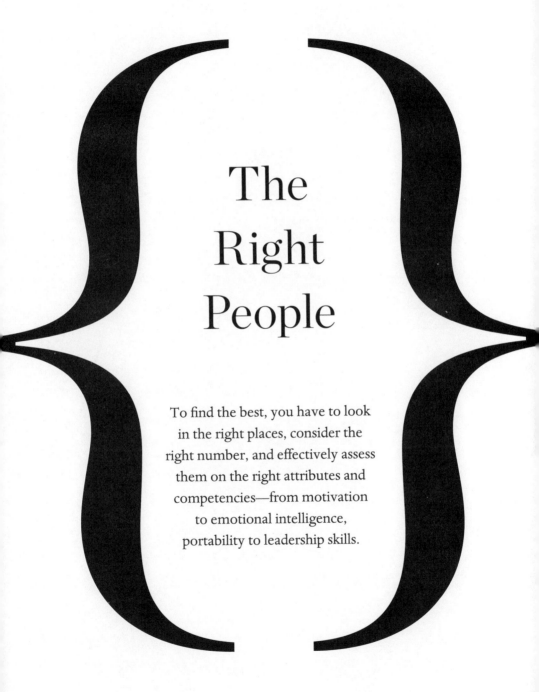

# PART THREE

# The Right People

To find the best, you have to look in the right places, consider the right number, and effectively assess them on the right attributes and competencies—from motivation to emotional intelligence, portability to leadership skills.

# The Magic Number

Back in 1611, Johannes Kepler's first wife died of cholera in Prague, ending an unhappy arranged marriage. The great astronomer then made a decision: instead of outsourcing his next marriage, he would systematically search for the right candidate. He made a list of eleven eligible women and carefully considered them for two full years. Eventually, he chose a favorite but was persuaded by friends to propose to someone else, the fourth woman on his list. Luckily, she turned him down, annoyed that he'd kept her waiting so long. Kepler returned to the one he really liked, and they lived happily ever after.

More than two centuries later, the famed evolutionary biologist Charles Darwin took a different approach to the same problem. Wondering whether to get married or not, he spent a few days writing down the pros and cons. After seeing that the former did indeed outweigh the latter, he began to consider potential candidates: colleagues, friends, acquaintances, family members. All of a sudden it came to him: his charming, intelligent, cultured cousin Emma would be perfect. He asked for her hand, they married and had children, and she proved to be an invaluable asset, both supporting his scientific work and tending to his numerous health problems. They too lived happily ever after.

The two scientists had dramatically different strategies for finding their mates. Kepler generated many candidates and evaluated them for two years; Darwin thought about his needs and picked just one who was a good fit very quickly.

So, how many candidates should you consider when making your crucial people decisions?

Many researchers have looked into this problem. Statisticians rely on probabilistic models, which are summarized in the "37 percent rule": if you have one hundred candidates, check the first thirty-seven to get a sense of what they all look like, and then from number thirty-eight on choose the first one that is better than all of the previous thirty-seven. Biologists can tell us how partnering animals make their choices: They first estimate their own attractiveness by getting feedback from members of the opposite sex. An offer from a good-looking potential mate might raise their level of aspiration; a rejection from an inferior one would lower it. After an "adolescence" involving some twenty interactions, they figure out which of their fellow species they can realistically aim for and settle down into stable relationships.[1]

In the real world, of course, we don't often consider one hundred or even twenty candidates. In fact, in many cases, we consider only one. According to research from the Center for Creative Leadership, this happens in nearly a quarter of executive appointments, and a study cited in Chip and Dan Heath's book *Decisive! How to Make Better Choices in Life and Work,* confirms that such decision making is rife in business.[2] Paul Nutt, a former Ohio State University professor who spent thirty years carefully analyzing 168 major corporate decisions, found that a full 71 percent were made after the executives responsible for them considered only a single alternative. Each choice was a binary one: whether or not to acquire that company, launch that product, enter that market, hire that person. And yet analysis showed that these "yes-or-no" scenarios led to poor outcomes 52 percent of the time, while the failure rate for decisions that involved two or more alternatives was only 32 percent.[3] Another study of eighty-three big decisions at a German technology firm showed that 40 percent of them were binary, even though choices between more alternatives were six times as likely to generate positive results.[4] Clearly, when trying to surround yourself with the best, it makes sense to consider several alternatives.

But you shouldn't overdo it, since there's also ample evidence that we react adversely to "choice overload." A classic study by Columbia University's Sheena Iyengar and Mark Lepper monitored the behaviors of grocery store customers who were confronted with a sample table of six different jams, or twenty-four. Amazingly, those shown the smaller set of jams were ten times more likely to actually buy a jar than those overwhelmed with twenty-four flavors.[5] Clearly, less is often more.

What's the magic number of candidates then? I worked with our firm's research center in India on a massive analysis to study the relationship between how many people we had presented to our clients in thousands of executive searches all over the world and the "stick rate" of the one hired—that is, how many years he or she had stayed at the company, either in the original position or moving up to a more senior role. My expectation was that a larger pool of people interviewed would increase the stick rate, and that happened up to a point. But after three or four candidates, it rapidly declined, confirming that too many options generate suboptimal decisions.

So three to four seems to be the right number, just as it is with the interviewers you involve in your key people decisions. But wait: Weren't Kepler and Darwin out of this range with their eleven and one candidates? How did they both end up in happy marriages? They compensated for respectively considering too many and too few potential mates with great people-selection strategies. Kepler cleverly sourced and rigorously assessed the best potential options. Darwin very clearly defined what he was looking for and, given his deep knowledge of his cousin Emma, had no doubt she was the right person to satisfy his needs. You can help yourself by getting the right number of people on your short list. But nothing replaces thorough preparation and evaluation.

# The Checklist Manifesto, Revisited

Before 1953, there was no standard procedure to determine if a newborn baby was in distress. The physicians in the room simply used their intuitive judgment, which unfortunately meant that danger signs were often missed, and many infants died. One day over breakfast, someone asked anesthesiologist Virginia Apgar how she might make these assessments more systematic. "That's easy," she replied. She jotted down five variables (heart rate, respiration, reflex, muscle tone, and color) and three scores (0, 1, 2). Babies would be rated one minute after they were born and their scores added up. Out of a maximum score of 10, 8 would mean a pink, crying, squirming, grimacing infant with a high pulse; 4 or less would mean one requiring immediate intervention. That Apgar test is now used in delivery rooms around the world every day.[1]

As surgeon and journalist Atul Gawande has expertly argued, checklists are essential to effective healthcare.[2] In my opinion, they are also critical to making great people choices. Two years after

Apgar's breakfast, in 1955, Daniel Kahneman was a twenty-one-year-old lieutenant in the Israeli Defense Forces with a daunting assignment: set up an armywide interview system. At the time, soldiers were chosen based on their performance in a battery of psychometric tests, as well as interviews with recruiters selected for their intelligence and people skills and trained to cover a range of topics. Unfortunately, these assessments proved useless, hence Kahneman's mandate.[3]

"I was no more qualified for the task than I was to build a bridge across the Amazon," reports the now famous psychologist, who won the 2002 Nobel Prize in Economics. But he had just read a wonderful book by the American psychology professor Paul Meehl, which showed how simple statistical rules produce much better predictions than intuitive judgments.[4] Meehl argued against broad, general evaluations and in favor of separately assessed attributes, so Kahneman devised a list of six characteristics that seemed relevant to performance in a combat unit, including *responsibility, sociability,* and even (in those days, for that army) *masculine pride.* For each factor, he developed questions about every candidate's life, delving into previously held jobs, punctuality, the frequency of his interactions with friends, his interest and participation in sports, and other issues. Interviewers were instructed to ask questions, listen to the answers, and then rate each attribute separately on a scale from 1 to 5. The simple sum of the six ratings turned out to predict soldiers' performance pretty well—way better than the old assessment model—and the army used Kahneman's process, virtually unchanged, for the next four decades.[5]

My best checklist story comes from the early 1990s, when Argentina went through a massive series of privatizations. This was a huge opportunity for me and our firm, since many large utilities needed to rapidly become much more efficient and market-oriented in order to survive and prosper. But it was also a huge challenge. I had to assess the top management at dozens of companies and quickly realized I would need a solid framework for conducting and communicating these reviews.

Armed with my MBA and McKinsey training, I came up with five attributes I thought would be useful: educational background, professional schools, results orientation, ability to organize, and team building and leadership. I decided to rate each separately and then average them to summarize my view on each manager's expected contribution. The results of this approach proved spectacular: virtually all appointments made following the appraisals had stick rates of higher than five years, and many of the chosen executives were further promoted to higher levels. And I still use the checklist approach today, albeit with a more customized and reliable set of competencies, to consistently achieve a success rate of about 90 percent in my hirings. As a result of that framework, I also became the founding leader of our firm's global management appraisal practice, which is now our second-largest source of revenue globally, and the head of our professional development team, which has involved training all our consultants in more than sixty offices around the world.[6]

How can you bring checklists into your own "who" decisions? In some of the chapters that follow, I'll discuss the importance of some general requirements, including potential, emotional intelligence, portability, and eight key leadership competencies. But you should also be as specific as possible about the job you need done. Write down the *essential* conditions necessary to perform it, such as speaking a certain language. Then, list *desirable* attributes you'd like to see in a candidate; this second category of "discriminating competencies" should be short, perhaps five or six items long, never more than ten. Next, rate each candidate on each factor, using a simple scale with no more than five levels. Finally, add the total score for each candidate, giving equal weight to each attribute, and choose the one with the highest score.

Take a look at a confidential report from any major executive search firm, and you'll always find some version of a checklist. Yes, there is some personal background and a work history but the most important part is the independent assessment of each candidate on each key competency, followed by a summary recommendation. Even boards of the world's largest companies pick their CEOs this way; and when they discuss with discipline how each candidate scores on the list, they make better choices, literally creating billions of dollars of value.

Many people greet this idea with skepticism. At one end of the spectrum, I'm asked why I don't advocate a more sophisticated process or complex algorithm that would give different weight to different attributes. But Kahneman himself says the most important development in this field of study since Meehl's original work is psychologist Robyn Dawes's article "The Robust Beauty of Improper Linear Models in Decision Making," in which he observes that complex statistical algorithms add little or no value; we can do just as well by selecting a set of scores that have some validity for predicting the outcome, and a simple equal-weight formula is likely to be as accurate in predictions as the optimal multiple-regression formula in the original sample.[7]

At the other end, I'm told that my cold calculation ignores the power of intuition. "You are turning us into robots!" people protest. Again, I refer them to Kahneman. To critics of his plan for the Israeli army, he said, "Carry out the interview as instructed and when you are done, have your wish: close your eyes, try to imagine the recruit as a soldier, and assign him a general score on a scale of 1 to 5."[8] These "intuitive" rankings were just as effective in predicting good candidates as the calculations of separate attributes—but only because they were made after the interviewers had been made to objectively consider (if not score) all those key skills. Checklists work.

# Nature versus Nurture

As baseball legends go, it's hard to top Ted Williams. With keen vision, quick wrists, and a scientific approach to hitting, he set all sorts of amazing records despite missing nearly five full seasons due to military service (where he also received an impressive series of medals and decorations).[1] He was the last player in the Major League with a season batting average over .400 (with a .406 in 1941) and, although he retired in 1960, he *still* holds the highest career batting average of anyone with five hundred or more home runs. Other accomplishments include two Triple Crowns, two MVP awards, six American League batting championships, seventeen All-Star game selections and, as the Hall of Fame would put it, "universal reverence."[2]

If you were a baseball coach, you'd love to sign a Ted Williams clone. If you're a big baseball fan, you know that might one day be a possibility. When Williams died of cardiac arrest at age eighty-three on July 5, 2002, his family decided to have his remains frozen (going against his stated desire to be cremated and have his ashes scattered in the Florida Keys, where he loved to fish). According to a story by Tom Verducci in *Sports Illustrated,* surgeons performed a postmortem "neuroseparation" (a much more refined version of those Dayak decapitations I described in chapter 14), and Williams's head and body are now stored in separate nitrogen-filled containers at an Arizona cryonics lab.[3] One daughter reported that the impetus for the procedure was her half-brother's desire to save and clone their father's DNA so "a lot of little Ted Williams [will be running] around the world 50 years from now."[4]

Assuming it's even possible, would it work? Would a Ted Williams clone really be as good a baseball player as the original? Was the greatest hitter who ever lived born or made? What about a voice like Celine Dion, a leader like Nelson Mandela, or a business genius like Bill Gates? There's no question that some people are innately exceptional. After all, Mozart learned to play the clavier between ages three and four years. More recently, Sunny Sanwar, who was born 1989, learned to draw museum-worthy portraits by age seven, and to fluently read, write, or speak six languages by age eight before finishing high school in eight months with honors. At the same time, others develop over time. Winston Churchill was labeled an unpromising youngster, Charles Darwin had trouble at school, and it took ages for little Albert Einstein to start to speak.

What can you change and what can't you—especially when you're dealing with fully formed adults? Early civilizations believed that we humans advanced only through God's grace, and that attitude continued through the Middle Ages. Perhaps not everyone subscribed to John Calvin's view that they were damned or saved before birth, but certainly very few thought they were masters of their own destinies. Sons did what their fathers did before, women were ignored, the poor remained poor, the rich stayed rich, and little knowledge was accumulated. The Enlightenment changed all that, of course, ushering in an era of science, education, and political freedom that shifted the prevailing wisdom toward the other end of the spectrum. People began to believe in human plasticity and, eventually, social mobility. Today, an entire self-help industry revolves around the idea that we can improve anything about ourselves—our bodies, our mind-sets, and all manner of skills from speed reading to public speaking, collaboration to negotiation—well into old age.

The truth lies somewhere in the middle. Sometimes nurture (or a good manager) can trump nature; sometimes it's the other way around. In Martin E. P. Seligman's book *What You Can Change . . . And What You Can't*, the father of positive psychology uses studies on identical twins separated at birth and other fascinating research to debunk many myths about change.[5] Among the (slightly demoralizing) highlights: dieting almost never works long-term, no treatment can improve on the natural course of recovery from alcoholism, and reliving childhood trauma does not undo adult personality problems. At the same time, Seligman shows that we can develop for the better in several key areas, including overcoming panic and sexual dysfunctions, controlling our moods, curing depression (using the right approach), and learning optimism.

To effectively evaluate and then develop people, you need to have a firm understanding of this idea. What can you change about yourself and the people around you, and what can't you?

*IQ*—that is, the level of general intelligence (including analytical, verbal, mathematical, and logical reasoning)—is pretty static for adults. You don't need to go out looking for geniuses since, for most jobs, there is a "threshold level" IQ needed, and anything above it has almost no impact on performance. However, you should still make sure to hire people clever enough for your requirements, because high general intelligence is an important asset (especially for knowledge workers), and you can't expect it to evolve dramatically over time. In some rare cases, you might measure for IQ. Mostly, though, you will have to rely on educational systems and early job experiences to filter for it and try to gauge it for yourself during interviews.

*Values* rarely change in adulthood. You need to check not only the essentials, such as honesty and integrity, which should be acid tests for any candidate you're considering, but also that the person shares your core values, since you can teach skills, but not character. As Jim Collins recounted in *Good to Great,* Nucor Steel made a point of hiring people from farming rather than steel towns, realizing that it would be easier to teach people to make steel than to imbue them with the farmers' work ethic.[6] Check whether applicants have in the past demonstrated altruistic values in practice—on the job and even in their personal activities.

*Motivation*—to excel, advance, grow and learn—is also typically there or not once people have progressed beyond their formative years. Combined with four key leadership attributes—curiosity, insight, engagement, and determination—motivation is a key indicator of potential, as I'll discuss in chapter 18.

Because these performance drivers are inherent or developed early, be sure to carefully check for all three as you talk to both candidates and their references.

{ 18 }

# From Survivor
# to CEO

Pedro Algorta's story is an unbelievable one. On October 13, 1972, he was flying over the frozen Andes, one of forty-five passengers on a twin-engine turboprop plane that had been chartered by a team of rugby players from his hometown of Montevideo, Uruguay. Suddenly, the plane hit frightening turbulence and pitched toward jagged mountain peaks. The pilots tried to recover altitude, but it was too late. One of the wings clipped a slope and was ripped off. The rest of the plane skidded to a stop on the soft snow of a glacier at an elevation of about twelve thousand feet. The impact instantly killed twelve people; five died from their injuries the next day. Among the casualties were four of Algorta's university classmates, including one of his best friends, who had joined him on the flight. And that was just the beginning of the twenty-one-year-old's ordeal—one of the most dramatic survival stories of the past two centuries.[1]

It has been chronicled in several books and one movie, *Alive,* but I'll briefly recount it here as well. The days were bitingly cold; the nights frigid, and endless. During one period of painful darkness, Algorta heard a blast in the distance and within seconds an avalanche engulfed the open end of the plane fuselage. He was buried alive, and as the snow started freezing, there was less and less oxygen to breath. Algorta realized he was dying. But then one of his fellow passengers removed the snow over his face, his lungs filled with air, and his fight for life continued.

There was no food other than wine and chocolate, which the group rationed for a few days. Through a small transistor radio that had survived the crash, they heard that they were only expected to last seventy-two hours and that, although search-and-rescue teams canvassed the Andes for ten days, they had ultimately been given up for dead.

Soon, the group started to discuss the unthinkable—eating the flesh of the frozen bodies around them. Algorta told his colleagues that their deceased comrades would surely consider it an act of love to help the rest survive and so eventually, with broken glass, they cut a few small pieces from one corpse, then ate them one by one. In this way, Pedro Algorta and fifteen others survived for seventy-two days before they were rescued.

Fourteen years later, in 1986, I hired Algorta into the Bemberg Group, by that time one of the largest industrial groups in Latin America. He started as a modest project manager at a small Quilmes beer brewery in Argentina's Corrientes province, and although he had zero experience in consumer goods, marketing, sales, or the region, he was spectacularly successful in the role. Soon, he became the general manager of the brewery, and not long after that he was promoted to CEO of Quilmes. Algorta was also a key member of the team that, under the leadership of the legendary Norberto Morita, successfully transformed the Bemberg Group from a quintessential family-owned enterprise to a large, respected conglomerate with managers considered to be among the best in the region.

I'll admit now that I got lucky hiring Algorta. In my early days as a search consultant, I didn't yet know how to effectively assess his potential for success. However, having watched him closely for thirty years and heard his firsthand account of that miraculous survival story, I now see why he has achieved so much. He had (and still has) the two hallmarks of someone with high potential: *the right motivation* and *four key leadership assets.*

Algorta has always had the right motivation: a blend of fierce commitment and deep personal humility. He wants to have a positive impact on others for the good of the larger group or organization. He gets satisfaction from seeing others succeed and values mission over personal reward. He showed this during his ordeal in the Andes by playing a critical yet very humble role, building the strength of the explorers who would eventually march out and save the group; he melted snow to quench their thirst and cut and dried small pieces of human meat to feed them. And he's displayed the same values throughout his career. Indeed, his ten-year stint with Bemberg came to an end only because, for sound strategic reasons, he recommended the group abandon the agribusiness project he was leading, voting himself out of his job.

Algorta also had the four key leadership assets common to all high-potential executives: *curiosity, insight, engagement,* and *determination.* There wasn't much to be curious or insightful about in the Andes, but Algorta took an interest in the water coming off the melting ice. It flowed east, leading him, and only him, to believe (rightly) that the dying pilot had misreported their position; they were on the Argentine side of the mountain range instead of the Chilean one. Algorta's engagement and determination were also clear over those seventy-two days. Ignoring the drama of death and agony surrounding him, he compassionately cared for and encouraged his companions. He faithfully remained by the side of his dying friend, Arturo Nogueira, who had suffered multiple fractures in his legs, bringing water and scraps of food and trying to distract the young man from his pain until he finally passed away. Algorta also persuaded his fellow survivors to promise that, should they die, they would condone the others using their bodies for sustenance.

Until he retired, Algorta brought all those same attributes to his executive work. He constantly sought new experiences, knowledge, and candid feedback; proactively gathered and made sense of information to map out new directions; used emotion and logic to communicate a persuasive vision and connect people; and fought toward difficult goals despite seemingly insurmountable challenges.

The right motivation and four key leadership attributes—curiosity, insight, engagement, and determination—allowed Algorta to survive the Andes and help fifteen others do the same. They also allowed him to grow into a great CEO.[2] To find the people with the highest potential to become the best, you have to look for those key indicators.

# Marshmallow Kids

Picture a four–year-old boy sitting at a table. An adult places a tasty marshmallow in front of him and tells him he has a choice. He can either eat it immediately or wait about fifteen minutes and get an extra marshmallow to enjoy. Then the adult leaves the room.

Put yourself in the boy's little shoes: a naked marshmallow in front of you and nobody is watching. What terrible temptation! Should you eat it? Can you possibly wait for the second one? Walter Mischel first conducted this experiment in the late 1960s with the children of some of his Stanford University colleagues, and it's been replicated many times since.[1] The results are typically as follows: About a third of kids grab the marshmallow and gulp it down as soon as the adult walks out the door. Another third try valiantly but ultimately fail to resist. (If you want a laugh, look for the YouTube videos documenting their techniques. Some cover their eyes or bury their heads in their arms; others sing songs, talk to themselves, or play games with their hands or feet. My favorite is the boy who picks up the marshmallow and puts it down; picks it up and puts it down; picks it up a third time, eats a tiny bit from the bottom, and then again puts it down to hide his transgression!) A final third of the kids are impressive: they hold out for two marshmallows.

What made Mischel's series of experiments extraordinary was not the initial split between the marshmallow eaters and resisters but what happened to those kids (he's followed more than six hundred) as they grew up. Those who had the willpower to delay gratification at age four were, as teenagers, more organized and effective, confident and assertive, trustworthy and dependable, resilient and self-reliant. In contrast, those who couldn't resist temptation were in adolescence more stubborn and argumentative, less decisive, easily irritated and upset by frustrations, and prone to jealousy. There was a clear difference in academic performance as well: the resisters' average college entrance exam scores were 210 points higher (out of a possible 1,600) than the eaters'. And as these kids became working adults, the success gap widened.

The "marshmallow test" happens to be an amazing predictor of future achievement because it measures self-control, a key aspect of what famed management theorist Daniel Goleman calls *emotional intelligence*. Indeed, I first read about Mischel's study in Goleman's classic 1995 book *Emotional Intelligence*.[2] I immediately contacted him to see how we might collaborate on research and spent the next seven years as part of a consortium that he coleads.

My first studies analyzed the profiles of a large sample of candidates my Egon Zehnder colleagues and I had hired into different positions around the world over the years, to see how EI affected performance. And the findings were striking: emotional intelligence was the most important predictor of success—ahead of experience, education, and IQ. When I hadn't properly assessed candidates to make sure they had these soft skills, they failed 25 percent of the time. When I did check, the failure rate was as low as 3 percent. Those conclusions applied everywhere, including the Americas, Europe, and Asia, though we found EI was even more crucial in volatile environments and for senior leaders.

What can you learn from the marshmallow kids and our follow-up research? Remember that no matter how "clever," experienced, and educated you are, you still have to work on managing yourself and your relationships with others. Also, when making your "who" decisions, you must carefully evaluate emotional intelligence. How self- and socially aware is your candidate? Does she show self-control? And how are her people skills, including leadership, influencing, teamwork, collaboration, conflict resolution, and change management?

Because these things are more difficult to assess than experience and academic accolades we tend to underestimate their importance. We hire people on the "hard," but we fire them for failing on the "soft." Don't make that mistake. In today's volatile, uncertain, complex, and ambiguous business world (VUCA is the US military acronym for it), the flexibility, adaptability, initiative, and resilience that come with EI are more crucial than ever. Only those who surround themselves with the right marshmallow kids (and show high emotional intelligence themselves) will be able to survive and thrive.

{ 20 }

# Fat Calves and
# Falling Stars

My wife, children, and I have a farm in beautiful and peaceful Patagonia, where we fatten cattle. Each fall we buy a few hundred calves recently separated from their mothers, and then keep them for eleven months, letting them feed on our natural grass. Once they've gained enough weight, we sell them and restart the cycle. The first year we did this, results were spectacular: the animals doubled their weight, and prices were sky-high. In the years that followed, we started buying calves from better farms but, for some reason, our average annual weight gain kept dropping, along with our revenues. And last year's selling season was our worst ever.

Puzzled, I asked a good friend, whose family has a three-generation history of breeding and fattening cattle in Patagonia, for advice. "Claudio, that first year when your animals gained so much weight, where did you buy them?" he asked me. I told him they came from a dry-land farm with very poor soil and low-quality grass. "See," he said. "That's what you want. If you find calves that can survive in a poor and hostile environment, the minute they get to your farm, they will blossom."

Last month I bought half of my cattle from a seller with low-quality grass, and a year from now I'll be able to tell you whether my friend's theory is right or not. But his insight makes a lot of sense—and it applies to human talent as well.

The best employees and executives are what talent management experts call *portable*. They are able to effectively transition from one role, company, industry, or country to the next, not only bringing their unique strengths to each but also growing stronger in the process. My great colleague and hero, Harvard Business School professor Boris Groysberg, is a pioneer in this field of research (indeed, his wife Liliya tells me that their youngest daughter's first word was *portability*), and each year when I visit HBS as a guest lecturer, I never miss a chance to watch him teach the subject to his students.[1]

Most people assume that the best hiring strategy is to find the best performers in a given field and get them on your team. But Boris and his colleagues have found that most people aren't so portable: some who are shining stars in one context can fall out of the sky in another. One of the best ways in which he demonstrates this is with a study on equity research analysts moving between Wall Street investment banks. You would expect high portability in these situations. As Boris puts it, when a star analyst at investment bank A accepts an offer to join investment bank B, he gets a box, puts his laptop and a few other things in it, goes down the elevator, looks left and right before crossing Wall Street, goes up the elevator, and exactly fifty-six seconds later he is working at his new job. He operates in a similar environment, analyzes the same companies in the same sector, and has the same clients. He doesn't have to sell his house, move to another state, buy a new house, look for new schools for the children, or help his spouse cope and adjust to a move. What could be easier? Yet, Boris has found that, while star equity research analysts that stay at one firm continue to shine, the performance of those who move declines quite dramatically in the following year and remains below previous heights even after five years.

Talent is much less portable than what we think because performance isn't just one "P"; it stems from five—processes, platforms, products, people, and politics—and most of those you can't take with you.

Am I, a twenty-eight-year veteran search consultant, confessing my sins and telling you that executives can't successfully move from one organization to another and so you shouldn't ever hire from the outside? Of course not. Sometimes it's the only alternative, or the best one. But you should help yourself make better decisions on outside hires, as well as internal moves, by learning the key lessons on talent portability. While falling stars are the *average* outcome, there are several caveats.

First, origin and destination matter. While cattle from fertile farms didn't gain as much weight at ours, the survivors of poor environments flourished. Likewise, when an executive moves to a weaker firm, performance is likely to decrease; if the person moves to a stronger firm, he or she will keep shining. Think about it in more practical terms: Should you embrace candidates only from outstanding firms like McKinsey or Goldman Sachs, as many companies do? Or would you be better off following a more counterintuitive strategy and finding the true stars who have managed to thrive at weaker firms?

Team-specific human capital is important too: when people move together, they tend to do better than when they do it alone. Boris has also found that starting something new in a new company (what he calls *exploration*) is much harder than taking over an existing project, team or unit (*exploitation*). In addition, some types of roles are more portable than others: COOs are much less portable because their job requires lots of internal knowledge and many relationships; CFOs and other functional experts are usually better positioned to move.

Finally, you must check for how well an incoming star will fit into your industry given its dynamics; your organization given its culture and strategy; and your team given the personalities on it. Consider the performance of GE executives hired to lead other companies. We all know that the company has long been a factory for talent, so much so that its alumni usually account for the largest group of CEOs within the *Fortune* 500.[2] Whenever an executive leaves GE to become the CEO of another firm, the market value of the latter typically spikes—by at least $1 billion for large entities, and in some cases by up to $10 billion.[3] Yet when Boris, along with Harvard Business School's Andrew N. McLean and Nitin Nohria, analyzed the performance of those stocks over the following three years, the results were mixed. While many of the newly appointed CEOs created great value, others presided over huge value destruction. What made the difference? Fit, and especially the strategic kind: some people are great for start-ups, others for turnarounds, others for managing cyclical businesses.

If you want to keep your stars bright, reject the myth of the executive who shines at all times and in all places. Instead, assess for your candidates' portability, including a careful check for fit.

# Why I Like People with Unconventional Résumés

Two years ago, I wrote a blog post for HBR.org called "Why I Like People with Unconventional Résumés."[1] In it, I argued that while professional success used to depend on experience, knowledge, and skill, things have changed a lot in recent decades. First, knowledge is both universally available and rapidly obsolete. Second, we live in an increasingly uncertain and volatile world (the VUCA conditions I described in chapter 19). And, finally, business has become more global and diverse.

In this new normal, job candidates with a penchant for personal disruption who have succeeded at big transitions should have a leg up on those who have followed traditional career paths because they've already proven they have the key factors that differentiate stars from average performers. As I explained in the last few essays, these include portability, several EI competencies (flexibility, adaptability, resilience, empathy, organizational awareness, and relationship management) and potential (the right motivation plus curiosity, insight, engagement, and determination). In my view, major job shifts suggest that a person is seeking learning, challenge, and growth and has the wherewithal to master new companies, sectors, cultures, and strategies.

To my surprise, that blog prompted more than three hundred passionate comments and became the month's most popular HBR piece. I also got hundreds of e-mails and, as you can imagine, a fair number of unconventional résumés for my consideration, including one from an active European government minister. I carefully went over all of them and found a phenomenal set of people with extraordinary achievements. And yet most of these correspondents told me that time and again, they had been frustrated by recruiters (internal and external) who didn't appreciate, understand, or even consider their track record. Some of the first comments on the blog include: "Love the point of view. Unfortunately I don't feel like that thinking is widespread in the industry" and "I would love to meet employers who think like you." Also: "It's too bad we don't have a job board/recruiter list of folks who thought like this. As a business owner, I'd jump at the chance to get these people on the team. As a job seeker, I'd also jump at the chance to work for a company that I knew would have me trying new things in twelve months. Seems like a win-win."

Then I started to feel guilty—because of course there have been many times in my career when I've accepted the safe choice and failed to defend an unconventional candidate who nevertheless had exceptional potential. I, too, have been a politically correct consultant when I should have been willing to play the role of "insultant," bravely challenging a client who favored bog-standard, over interesting, experience. I wish I'd hired more Pedro Algortas (from chapter 18), who became such a success at Bemberg despite lacking the industry, functional, and regional background needed for his first role at the company.

But I am emboldened now. As I said in that blog post, I'm convinced we're entering a new era of talent selection. When I joined the search profession back in the 1980s, we focused on performance. The mantra was that "the best predictor of future success is past success." That worked well until jobs started to become more dynamic. We then started assessing competencies, decomposing all the new and varied jobs into their essential parts and assessing candidates on each one. Today, identifying potential should be our first priority, and people who have already thrived in nonlinear careers form an excellent candidate pool.

At Egon Zehnder, we never hire anyone who has worked for another executive search firm, because we care enormously about taking a completely different approach to the profession; all of us have completely different backgrounds (in my case, operations and logistics followed by management consulting with McKinsey). But we never compromise on values, cultural fit, and potential.

In client work and elsewhere, the list of extraordinary people with unconventional résumés I've met is striking:

- A good friend of mine from northern Europe was trained during the Cold War to become either a spy or an interrogator and learned Russian. Although he had no undergraduate degree, he applied for and was amazingly accepted into an Ivy League business school. He went on to become chairman and CEO of one of the world's finest global professional service firms.

- Another friend used to be a pilot in the Argentine navy. He joined McKinsey, which put him through an accelerated graduate program in management. One of the firm's clients, a beverage company, hired him in spite of his lack of line experience. He was eventually promoted to lead the group's Latin America business from Brazil.

- I recently had the pleasure of meeting someone hired five years ago to be director of procurement for CAPEX (capital expenditures) projects at a major global resources company, responsible for an annual budget of more than $50 billion. He had no background at all in the procurement function, yet his employer recognized his potential. Today, he leads one of the firm's largest and most important global divisions.

As the iconic ad-man and agency founder David Ogilvy asserted, "It sometimes pays to be imaginative and unorthodox in hiring." He himself joined the industry as a copywriter at age thirty-nine, after stints working in a hotel kitchen, living among the Amish, and trying door-to-door sales.

When managing your own career, make sure to expose yourself to new experiences and challenges rather than just moving up the ladder. Seek out people who will help you do this. And when evaluating others in your quest to surround yourself with the best, don't stop at checking their past experience and performance (which matter) and their competencies (which matter even more). Also consider *potential*, which is the real key to lasting success in our fast-changing, globalized world. And never automatically discount someone whose job history differs from the norm. In fact, give them a close look. Versatility is a huge asset.

# Lightbulbs and CEOs

Imagine that you light a thousand identical lightbulbs, all from the same producer, and leave them on until they burn out. Inevitably, one will last longer than all others, and yet no one could predict which one it would be. Some people think the same is true of executives, including CEOs: luck is the reason a few outperform, and yet they are held up as shining examples for the rest of us.

When I first heard that argument a decade or two ago, my first reaction was to scoff. Of course, we all know that some people are more gifted and motivated than others; I've based my career on that premise. But my second, less primitive decision was to study the best research on the topic. Is leadership success based on luck? Or was Jim Collins right in saying, "Whether you prevail or fail, endure or die, depends more on what you do to yourself than on what the world does to you"?

Statisticians have come up with a very clever way to untangle skill and luck. In a model called *true score theory*, they use the distribution of outcomes in any given activity to determine how much is generated by true ability and how much by pure randomness.

Consider a few sports. In basketball, luck accounts for only 12 percent of results, while in hockey, it is as high as 53 percent. In men's tennis, where each player hits the ball some six hundred times in a best-of-five match, luck plays a very small role.

Moving from sports to executive performance, studies show that luck does have an impact. In his book *The Success Equation: Untangling Skill and Luck in Business, Sports, and Investing*, Michael J. Mauboussin refers to research conducted by Andrew Henderson at the University of Texas, who worked with Deloitte Consulting to understand the patterns of performance in more than 20,000 companies over a forty-year period. In one analysis, they examined 228 companies featured in thirteen popular books on high performers and found that fewer than 25 percent could confidently be described as such. As they put it, "We suspect that a number of the firms that are identified as sustained superior performers based on five-year or ten-year windows may be random walkers . . . "[1]

At the same time, in other work, the researchers found there were more companies with sustained superior performance than pure luck could explain. In other words, while many of the popular theories for building lasting greatness are not valid, corporate success is clearly not "all about luck." Another great study proving this was conducted by Harvard Business School's Noam T. Wasserman, Nitin Nohria, and Bharat N. Anand. They found that about a third of organizational performance could not be explained statistically and was thus attributable to random effects. But four factors did matter. The strength of the company explained almost 33 percent of the variance; the industry, 15.5 percent; the CEO, 13.5 percent; and the year, just 5.2 percent. So leadership is not only a significant factor (the figure was 13.5 percent on average but as high as 40 percent in some markets) but also the most controllable one.[2] You can't do anything about the year or the economy; it's very hard to switch industries; and corporate change initiatives take huge effort and time. By contrast, executive appointments are much easier and faster to implement.

So far, so good. The right leaders can help a company make its own luck. But how do you find those people? How do you separate the skilled individuals from the lucky ones and, going back to our lightbulb analogy, identify the best CEOs, managers, and staff without burning through them all?

For some simple jobs, such as those on an assembly line, where success stems almost entirely from skill and motivation, this is easy: you can test all the candidates, measuring the number of items they can process per hour as a proxy for who will perform best on the job. For more complex roles, in which an individual's performance can be hurt or helped by many other factors, luck plays a larger part and the assessment is tougher. But it's not impossible if you know what to look for.

As I already explained, you first need to consider intelligence, values, the key indicators of potential (including motivation), emotional intelligence, and portability. But based on decades of executive search and management appraisal work, we at Egon Zehnder believe there are also eight leadership competencies that can predict executive success across all roles, sectors, and countries. While each job and organization is different, requiring different levels of mastery in each, these are skills that all the best people have in some measure:

- *Strategic orientation:* An ability to engage in broad, complex analytical and conceptual thinking

- *Market insight:* A strong understanding of the market and how it affects the business

- *Results orientation:* A commitment to demonstrably improving results

- *Customer impact:* A passion for serving the customer

- *Collaboration and influencing:* An ability to work effectively with peers or partners, including those not in the line of command

- *Developing organizational capability:* A drive to improve the company by attracting and developing top talent

- *Team leadership:* Success in focusing, aligning, and building effective groups

- *Change leadership:* An ability to drive change through people, transforming and aligning an organization around a new goal

The importance of these eight competencies was confirmed in a wonderful joint study that cross-referenced our database of more than a hundred thousand appraisals with McKinsey's growth statistics on more than seven hundred companies to create a sample of forty-seven companies with 5,560 ratings of their senior leaders.[3] The top-level finding was unequivocal: companies with higher levels of growth had executives with higher levels of competence in *every single one* of the areas we analyzed. Skill does indeed matter as much, if not more, than luck.

That said, many of the executives weren't outstanding across the board. Only 1 percent in the study sample achieved an average competency score of 6 or 7 out of 7, and only 11 percent were scaled 5 or higher. Nobody's perfect. So when looking to surround yourself with the best, your strategy should be to look for above-par skill in most categories and then stand-out competency in just the two or three areas that will be most important for your new hire. Carefully ask yourself: What is this specific job really about? What are the organizational conditions? Which of the eight competencies (or others) will differentiate the best performers from the rest in this case? How has this person demonstrated those skills in similar circumstances in the past?

Of course, it doesn't hurt to also hope for a bit of luck!

# Reading People
# around the World

They say that an Argentine is an Italian who speaks Spanish, pretends to be British, and likes to live in Paris. I was born in Buenos Aires, where we've always been keen observers of the rest of the world, particularly Europe and North America. I grew up speaking Spanish but studied English, French, and Latin at school, then learned Portuguese and Italian through work experience, so I can now comfortably read and communicate in five languages. Each year I circle the globe some ten times for executive search and speaking engagements, repeatedly visiting forty different countries.

As I write this, I've just returned from a marathon of lectures in Hong Kong, Shenzhen, and Beijing, and I'm soon heading for another one in Indonesia, Malaysia, and Singapore before I return to the East Coast of the United States for a teaching session at Harvard Business School, followed by a trip to the Middle East. The month this book comes out, I'm scheduled to give a keynote address at our firm's fiftieth-anniversary conference in Switzerland, attended by all colleagues who will have flown in from sixty-eight offices around the world.

*New York Times* columnist Thomas Friedman was certainly accurate when he argued that globalization is making the world "flat." But, as a frequent traveler, I also see that cultural differences still abound. And, everywhere I go, people ask me for advice on how to deal with them: "How do I read and assess people from diverse backgrounds? Does it take different abilities to lead successfully in different countries? Can you transplant people from one culture to another? How can my firm preserve its corporate ethos across markets while still acknowledging local customs?" These are the burning questions being asked at the world's biggest companies, and by any manager who wants to surround him- or herself with the best in our new, global world of work.

National cultures have distinct values, which in turn create different behaviors. There are many ways of mapping these but I like the model developed by the Dutch researcher Geert Hofstede, which analyzes five dimensions:[1]

- *Power distance* reflects the willingness of weaker members of organizations to accept an unequal distribution of power; it is quite high in Latin America, Africa, Asia, and the Arab world, and very low in Anglo and Germanic countries.

- *Individualism* measures the degree to which the person is distinguished from the group; North America and Europe are highly individualistic, while Asia, Africa, and Latin America have much stronger collectivistic values.

- *Uncertainty avoidance* indicates tolerance for ambiguity; it is quite high in Latin America, many southern and eastern European countries, and Japan and lower for Anglo, Nordic, and Chinese cultures.

- *Masculinity* scores the distribution of roles across genders; Japan and several European countries rank as highly masculine, while Nordic countries are much less so.

- *Long-term orientation* shows whether people focus on distant rather than immediate outcomes; it is high in East Asia, moderate in Europe, and low in the Anglo countries, the Muslim world, and Latin America.

As you can imagine, these differences, and the way people conduct themselves as a result of them, have massive implications in a business context, significantly complicating people decisions.

Given all the disparity, how can you possibly evaluate someone whose culture differs from your own or decide between two people from dramatically different parts of the world? Luckily, it's not that hard, because the list of skills required to be a successful leader anywhere in the world is actually quite universal. Research by our firm and the practices of virtually all major successful multinationals bear this out. Again, the list includes intelligence; values; key indicators of potential including motivation; emotional intelligence; portability; and eight specific leadership competencies (strategic orientation, market insight, results orientation, customer impact, collaboration and influencing, developing organizational capability, team leadership, and change leadership). It's possible to assess people anywhere in the world using this common language.

Of course, trying to evaluate diverse candidates on these isn't always easy. As I frequently joke, if I am assessing an Argentine and someone from Japan on results orientation, I would probably divide by two whatever achievements my conational passionately boasts about in Buenos Aires, while multiplying by two what the Japanese candidate in Tokyo is softly telling me, after several questions, looking down!

If you're unsure about the nuances of a particular culture, enlist an adviser who understands them. Egon Zehnder consultants always conduct management appraisals in pairs. One person—fully knowledgeable about the client company and the position that needs to be filled—is a constant in all interviews and travels around the world to participate in every meeting. The second consultant is a local of the country where the candidate is from or would be based. With both perspectives, we get an accurate interpretation of answers and behavior, a proper understanding of the potential cultural fit, and a realistic benchmarking against other local and global contenders.

If you don't have international colleagues or a global search firm to use for this purpose, consultants, auditors, and lawyers in the relevant country or region can be quite useful as advisers. They will drastically increase the quality of your assessments across cultures, and allow you to capitalize on the wonderful upside of globalization.

PART FOUR

# The Bright Future

Surrounding yourself with the best doesn't stop at selection. Your stars need the right integration, development, coaching, and promotion if you want them to truly shine.

# { 24 }

# Accelerated Integration

Every day, thousands of patients around the world receive organ transplants. Those who do are extremely lucky—in the United States alone, more than 100,000 people are waiting for the body parts they need to live—but they also face a significant chance of organ rejection, since the body's immune system is built to fight off any foreign presence.[1] A full 40 percent of transplanted lungs, for example, fail within the first year of surgery. Doctors simply can't guarantee success. However, there are three things they do to minimize the risk of failure: check for organ health, check for compatibility, and properly monitor and support the process before, during, and after the transplant.

When a new person joins your team or takes on a new role, there is a similar threat of rejection, and the strategies for success are the same. In the previous two parts, I discussed the first two imperatives for successful hires: to find the right people (healthy organs) and ensure they fit into your organization (compatibility). The third imperative is to properly support their integration.

Unfortunately, most of us don't do this, leaving those people we've chosen vulnerable. In a survey of participants in a recent Harvard Business School executive program on talent management, 95 percent listed managing stars as a top challenge for their companies, while fewer than 30 percent said it was one their organizations were equipped to overcome. Indeed, when Boris Groysberg carefully studied the integration practices of companies, he found that fewer than 4 percent devote enough resources to them.[2]

And yet, the benefits of effective integration are huge. According to Michael D. Watkins, author of the definitive guide to job transitions, *The First 90 Days*, the return on investment is in the order of 400 percent.[3] Focus on it with your people and you will accelerate their learning process, reduce their risk of failure, and boost both their short- and long-term performance.

Start by familiarizing yourself with the best practices Watkins outlines, including tools and strategies for achieving early wins and gaining credibility.[4] Surgeons study up on the latest and most successful techniques; you should too.

Prepare your organs before transplant as Pierre Delaere, a surgeon at the University Hospitals Leuven in Belgium, learned to do with tracheas. His breakthrough idea involved putting a donated windpipe into a woman's arm for a few years before moving it to her throat so her body would get used to it and cover it with its own cells, preventing rejection.[5] You can help a newcomer in the same way by ensuring he or she learns as much as possible about your team and organization's goals, stakeholders, and culture before he starts. Share critical information on governance, structure, and processes and agree on immediate priorities and long-term aspirations.

In the early days, make sure that people new to your company or those you've put in new positions—your transplants—are working effectively, and then monitor ongoing health, just as doctors do. Encourage them to meet with everyone who will play a role in their success (or failure). Outreach should be in five directions—*up* (to you and other bosses), *across* (to peers), *down* (to subordinates), *out* (to clients), and *in* (to personal contacts, such as family members and friends)—in search of advice on how to excel. After thirty days, evaluate their progress; after ninety days, consider lining up a 360-degree review; and, from then on for a year, check in monthly.

I recently participated in the annual partners' meeting of one of the most successful private equity groups in the world. The value of its portfolio companies has more than doubled in under five years, and not one has generated a significant loss over the past decade, pushing the annual rate of return to something on the order of 20 percent. The firm's strategy has always been to focus not on a company's sector or price (the "what") or the strategic transformation it needs (the "how") but on which people will make the investment a successful one (the "who"). This often involves upgrading the existing management team, which can be hard, particularly in cases where previous owners or founders and employees loyal to them remain. The secret to the partners' success? They carefully guide the transition process, speaking or meeting weekly with key stakeholders from both the original and new teams, for at least a year after an investment is made. Any top new executive also gets a monthly lunch date with a managing partner. Such steps require discipline and planning. But they are well worth the time and energy—and a lot less complex and expensive than postoperative organ care!

# Sophie's Choice

When you pick one person—to be your business partner, fill a critical position on your team, take on a key client or assignment—you are inevitably saying no to someone else. These decisions become particularly fraught if your organization is one that fast-tracks some executives into high-potential (HIPO) programs and you're responsible for nominating certain employees or peers over others. "It's like *Sophie's Choice*," Nitin Nohria, the dean of Harvard Business School, once told me.

Now, I'll admit that only he—the head of the world's most prominent management school—could get away with comparing the tensions of talent selection to the William Styron novel (and later Meryl Streep film) about a concentration camp prisoner having to decide which of her small children will be gassed to save the other.[1] But for those of us who care deeply about making great people choices, these evaluations can indeed be extremely difficult.

We rightly want to invest more time, attention, and resources in those whom we believe to have the most potential for growth. But that of course means limiting opportunities given to everyone else and potentially demoralizing the vast majority of solid contributors. As a result, many companies and leaders simply don't make tough choices, instead treating all employees the same, or letting them self-select into development.

As John Gardner, former secretary of health, education and welfare in the United States and the founder of Common Cause, so eloquently put it, "We can't be excellent and equal."[2] The question isn't whether or not to anoint high-potentials but how to do it in a sound and credible way that minimizes resistance, cynicism, and demotivation from the rest.

Using annual appraisals to make the first cut brings more objectivity to the process. But that's not enough, because those assessments are typically focused on performance and, while research from the Corporate Leadership Council and several others has demonstrated that all high-potentials are high performers, it also shows that most high performers are not high-potentials.[3] In other words, there are many more people who excel in their current jobs than there are people who will also be able to grow into larger and more complex roles. Therefore, as a second cut, I also recommend soliciting subjective views from peers and supervisors that specifically address the most valid and reliable indicators of potential, as I've described in chapter 18: the right motivation plus curiosity, insight, engagement and determination.[4]

You should also explicitly measure these things through behavioral interviews and references. Over the years, as our firm honed its model for assessing potential, we have often gone back to clients to compare our evaluations with the career evolutions of the executives we considered. Our conclusion is that the right assessor using the right model can learn to predict success (as measured by the number of promotions an executive gets over time) with significant accuracy. Unfortunately, however, surveys of Harvard Business School executive program participants indicate that, when it comes to selecting HIPOs, most organizations don't use a valid model and don't properly train their assessors.

Once you've identified people with potential, then you must carefully communicate your choice. This is a delicate topic: if you're completely open, you have to prepare for the disappointment of those not on the list, and even the frustration of high-potentials whose expectations are not met. For this reason, many organizations try to "hide" their classifications, as if that were possible. An early study on such practices conducted by Anthony J. Fresina & Associates in 1987 found that 78 percent of companies did not inform HIPOs of their designation, but 90 percent of the time employees found out anyway.[5] Meanwhile, the organizations that were more forthright about their development plans saw better retention and productivity. I strongly believe that transparency wins over secrecy. If your process is thorough, sound, and fair, you should be able to defend it. In private discussions, tell people when they've been fast-tracked so they know they're prized by you and the organization and encouraged to live up to the high standards being set for them. Tell everyone else—all those key workers who keep the clocks ticking and the trains running—that you value them too. Treat them well, pay them well, and continue to lead and motivate them.

Tough decisions are what make you a leader. As Jeff Bezos said in a May 2010 Princeton University commencement address, "In the end, we *are* our choices."[6] So don't shy away from embracing, protecting, and nurturing the best of the best, even when it means devoting less attention to the rest. These might not be life-or-death decisions, like Sophie's, but they are essential for building a bright future.

# {26}

# Teaching a Turkey
# to Climb a Tree

My friend Lyle Spencer, a world authority on talent selection and development, has a favorite saying: "You can train a turkey to climb a tree. But I'd rather hire a squirrel." Generally, I agree with him. After all, I've made my living helping companies find their squirrels—that is, executives whose experience, knowledge, and skills make them perfectly suited to our clients' needs. But I never discount the turkeys that show potential. With the right support, some can indeed learn to climb as far and as fast.

For a full decade, in parallel with my executive search activity, I led the internal professional development efforts at Egon Zehnder, creating and implementing all sorts of leadership training, education, and coaching initiatives across sixty-eight offices in forty countries. I also spent lots of time personally mentoring some of my colleagues and, as a member of the global executive committee, weighed in on scores of assignment and promotion decisions. And I've of course participated in hundreds of client searches and appointments, tracking the careers of thousands of managers. In that time, I've seen some remarkable stories of personal growth.

Let me start, humbly, with my own. I joined our firm at age thirty, from McKinsey. Highly analytical, shy, and introverted, I was absolutely short of the deep relational skills that executive search consultants—and leaders—need to succeed. Luckily, I was enrolled in an early training on influencing skills, so essential for the high-stakes, emotionally charged situations I would later face: encouraging a manager content in his job to switch, for example, or convincing a company owner to make a drastic change affecting his longtime employees. Through the program, I got some rich 360-degree feedback, which showed that my tendency to always emphasize logic (which is highly persuasive to me) was a problem in some situations, since it can have very little, or even negative, impact on other personality types. I was then introduced to a much wider array of influencing tactics (including modeling, appealing to values, consulting, negotiating, socializing, alliance building, and others) and I became much better at choosing the right one for each situation and person.

Another example comes from a former financial trader hired to be CFO of a consumer goods company. Brilliant at finding problems, spotting risks, investing, and reducing costs, he was highly respected for his financial expertise and had all the indicators of high potential. But he would ridicule his peers in public and had problems integrating with the larger organization. Eventually, he was sent to a leadership training program that, for the first time, made him aware of his shortcomings and much more open to others' points of view. He worked with a personal coach for two years, became CEO of the company and is now beloved by his team.

There's another old saying: *You can't teach an old dog new tricks.* But as these examples and reams of scientific research show, that's simply not true. Growing up, I used to believe that we were born with a huge amount of brain cells, which we would steadily lose until the day we died. I boxed as a young man and remember being horrified when I read about the number of cells killed with each punch to the head. Thankfully, I looked further and found some good news: every day, in a process called *neurogenesis,* the brain creates some ten thousand stem cells that split into two. One of them becomes a daughter line that continues producing stem cells, while the other migrates, quite often wherever it's needed in the brain for new learning. Over the next four months or so, that new cell forms some ten thousand connections with others, to create new neural circuits. Just think about those numbers: ten thousand new cells times ten thousand new connections per cell create 100 million new connections *per day.*[1] So our brains are ready to learn new tricks—including tree-climbing—at any age. The key is to focus on learning—and teaching—the right skills.

When training the people around you to do bigger and better things, which competencies matter most? Depending on your circumstances, you'll want to place more weight on some of the eight specific hallmarks of great leaders I set out in chapter 22. (I'll discuss this again in chapter 28.) But, in my experience, it also pays to concentrate more generally on emotional intelligence—either self-management (such as flexibility and adaptability, or emotional self-control) or relationship management (such as influencing others, dealing with conflict, or promoting change).

You might think that these "soft" skills would be harder to teach than hard ones such as calculus or coding. But research from another of my big heroes, Richard Boyatzis, at the Weatherhead School of Management (WSOM), Case Western Reserve University, shows otherwise.[2] Dismayed by studies of MBA programs indicating that students had increased their EI competencies by only 2 percent in the one to two years they were enrolled (compared with an average increase of 40–50 percent for all the competencies assessed), Boyatzis set out to change the status quo. In the fall of 1990, Weatherhead implemented a revised MBA course that included (1) a course on leadership assessment and development; (2) a focus on specific EI competencies in selected subjects, such as presentation skills in a marketing course or collaboration in an operations management course; (3) a dramatic increase in the number of courses requiring field work in companies and group projects; and (4) more opportunities to participate in volunteer activities and clubs. The results have been extraordinary: full-time MBAs saw their self-management skills improve by 47 percent, and their relationship-management ones by as much as 75 percent. Part-time MBAs, who take three to five years to complete their programs, meanwhile saw increases of 67 percent and 40 percent. This last group was assessed two years after graduating, and their level of emotional competence had remained at the new high level, confirming that the positive change was not only impressive but also lasting.

To develop the people around you without a formal MBA course, I suggest the following steps.[3]

First, make sure they really want to improve and have a strong vision of their desired future. When there is a will, there is a way, but without it, nothing will be achieved. Research on the neuroscience of behavioral change shows that *positive emotional attractors* focused on one's individual strengths and hopes arouse the parasympathetic nervous system, making us more calm, compassionate, and open to learning.

Second, help your people objectively assess their strengths and weaknesses and find the gaps between their "real selves" and their "ideal selves." Some form of 360-degree feedback becomes invaluable here.

Third, develop a learning agenda or action plan to close those gaps. This must be highly focused and practical. Don't try to change too much at once. Encourage people to work on specific behaviors and set incremental goals.

Fourth, encourage your learners to relentlessly practice their new behaviors so their brains develop a new neural circuitry that makes these better habits feel natural and automatic. This may take three to six months; they shouldn't get frustrated.

As a leader who wants to be surrounded by the best, you need to get your people inspired about improving themselves, especially when it comes to emotional competencies—to understand where they stand and where they fall short of ideal; to develop a clever change plan; and to persevere in practice. Turkeys can't learn to climb trees all by themselves!

# Growth from
# Complexity

When my first book, *Great People Decisions,* was published in Japan, I worked with my colleague Ken Aramaki from Egon Zehnder's Tokyo office on some country-level analysis. We mapped the *potential* of senior Japanese executives (that is, objective assessments from our search consultants about their ability to take on bigger roles and responsibilities, as measured by the indicators I listed in chapter 18) against their *competence* (that is, objective assessments on the eight leadership competencies I outlined in chapter 22), and then compared those scores to the average achieved by all executives in our worldwide database.

What we found was an incredible paradox. Japanese professionals had *higher potential* than the global average but *lower competence*. In spite of great raw material, there was a poor final product. The problem was, and still is, Japan's flawed refinement process. Although the country's educational institutions and cultural work ethic give its managers a jump-start in their careers, companies typically don't continue the development process as far as it could go.

How does a leader traditionally emerge in Japan? He rises through the ranks of one division, in one company, waiting respectfully for promotions that usually come only when he's the most senior person, with the longest tenure, in line for the spot. Recently, I became aware of the case of a Tokyo-based global conglomerate with a highly diversified business portfolio that could not find even one qualified CEO successor. This company, which stretched into all sorts of industries and markets, offering numerous strategic challenges, should have been an ideal training ground for executives. However, only one of its senior managers had worked in more than a single business line. The top twelve leaders had spent an average of just one year working outside of Japan. And their English language skills were quite limited. In sum, none were suitable candidates to succeed the CEO. The sad thing is that all of them had started off strong: they were engineers with an average tenure of more than twenty years in R&D and product strategy and marketing. But that potential had been squandered.

The fact is that giving people bigger jobs with fancier titles and larger salaries won't make them better. More *complex* assignments will. Just look at the leaders of ANZ, the global banking group headquartered in Melbourne. Each time an employee identified as having high potential is promoted, the company makes sure it's not to the same job on a larger scale (in terms of budget and resources) but to an entirely new set of challenges—maybe it's relocating to a new country, shifting from a staff to a line role, or moving from a turnaround situation to launching a new business unit. Companies like GE, Unilever, and McKinsey do the same, exposing their highest-potentials to new sectors, new companies, new markets, new situations, and new functions, making themselves leadership factories in the process.

Consider the trajectory of Marcelo Martínez Mosquera. After earning a degree in industrial engineering, he joined Techint, a multinational conglomerate with headquarters in Milan and Buenos Aires whose CEO, Paolo Rocca, also shows up in the Hansen, Ibarra, and Peyer list of the world's best CEOs at number 23.[1] Immediately recognized as a high-potential, Martínez Mosquera was exposed to new realities and complexities with every single early assignment. He was successively rotated through financial, commercial, marketing, and even production roles that exposed him to not only his domestic Argentine market but also the United States, key European clients, and even the opening of exports to Russia and China. All that equipped him to handle the very critical and delicate task of launching a new business that would compete with the company's clients. Not surprisingly, he was able to do it and quickly become one of the most senior leaders in the group.

If you want to really help the people around you, you have to make sure they have access to similar opportunities, even if the changes are on a smaller scale. Consider the six leadership passages brilliantly described by *The Leadership Pipeline* authors Ram Charan, Stephen Drotter, and James Noel: from managing yourself to managing others; from managing others to managing managers; from managing others to functional manager; from functional manager to business manager; from business manager to group manager; and finally, for those reaching the very top, from group manager to enterprise manager.[2] Can you help your people make those transitions? Also look for short-term, project-based assignments that will allow them to stretch and find new muscles. What interesting and challenging work can you give them access to—and then coach them through?

Don't make the mistake that many corporations do, even in some of the world's greatest nations like Japan. Remember that potential should trump seniority and that—when it comes to the jobs that help leaders grow most—complexity always beats size.

# Finding Alignment

Throughout this book, I've endeavored to surprise you with new research or stories in every chapter. But there's one study I discussed earlier to which I now must return. Remember that joint analysis from Egon Zehnder and McKinsey in chapter 22. The broad conclusion was straightforward: high-growth companies had executives with higher ratings in all eight key leadership competencies we analyzed, on average. However, there were some interesting subtleties in the findings.[1]

First, there was one skill that seemed more important than the rest in driving performance: customer impact. In companies that ranked in the top quartile for revenue growth, at least 40 percent of the senior executives scored 5 or above in this competency.

At the same time, my colleagues noticed that some of the most effective leaders had "spiky" ratings—extremely high in just two or three areas but barely average or even below average in others. Rather than trying to be the best at everything, they had focused on becoming truly brilliant in some competencies instead of trying to overcome their deficiencies in others.

Third, collective competency mattered more than individual stars. A small group of high-scoring executives—or a knock-it-out-of-the-park CEO—didn't drive business success. In fact those exceptional people were quite rare: as I mentioned before, only 1 percent of the more than 5,500 executives in the sample had an average competency score of 6 or 7 out of 7 and only 11 percent had an average score of 5 or higher. Instead, the best-performing companies had a critical mass of strong (if not outstanding) leaders.

Fourth, companies with different strategies excelled with different types of executives at different levels. Organic growth required a strong cadre of senior managers (i.e., not the top team) who shone at not only customer impact but also developing organizational capability, team leadership, and change leadership. Inorganic (M&A) growth was, by contrast, driven primarily just by top teams who excelled at market insight, results orientation, and strategic orientation, in addition to customer impact.

What lessons should you take from all this? To be extremely focused in your development efforts. Surrounding yourself with the best involves (1) understanding and building on each person's spiky strengths (giving some additional weight to customer impact), (2) ensuring that team members have skills that complement each other, making the whole greater than the sum of its parts, and (3) training your leaders in competencies that match their career stage and your team, unit or organization's broader goals.

It might be tempting to try to make everyone good at everything once you've brought them in. But that's a fool's errand because it requires a huge amount of time and investment to help even one smart, hardworking person improve in just one area. In our firm's experience, high-potential executives who receive intensive coaching and development support from their employers can boost their appraisal scores (on a scale from 1 to 7) by no more than +2 in one competency, or +1 in two, in one year. And no one can repeat this kind of improvement year after year. So it's much more effective to concentrate on the competencies in which your people stand the best chance of getting better, and those that offer the greatest benefits to your team, depending on your business and strategy.

Consider three case studies of companies that carefully matched their executive training programs to their respective situations: a turnaround, organic growth, and M&A.

- After a near-bankruptcy in 2002, Swiss engineering firm ABB realized that its state-of-the-art products were not enough. To achieve profitable growth, the company would need to better understand customers' needs. So in 2004 it created a leadership development plan for thousands of senior managers that emphasized three competencies: *customer impact*, *people development*, and *change leadership*. Participants were assessed by supervisors, peers, and reports; given improvement goals; reviewed on their progress; and compensated accordingly. A similar program was then rolled out to middle managers. The company has since seen impressive growth, and its people pipeline is stronger than ever. Instead of having only 30 percent of vacancies in its top two hundred roles filled by internal candidates, the figure is now 85 percent.

- Confronted with heavy competition and global expansion goals, a major pharmaceutical company invited cohorts of forty managers at a time to participate in skill-building workshops and field projects focused on *customer impact*, *team leadership*, *developing organizational capability*, and *change leadership*. The work included a plan to relaunch a key product in emerging markets; proposals for diversifying into new services; and a recommendation to reshape the company's customer interaction model by cutting the sales force by 25 percent and reinvesting the savings in other marketing channels. This practical, focused leadership development had a big impact: within eighteen months, more than 90 percent of the participants had been promoted and the company's profits are on the rise.

- Having made more than a hundred acquisitions over the past decade, US technology giant IBM is unabashed in emphasizing the importance of *market insight, strategic orientation,* and *results orientation* to its executives. The motto "THINK" was coined by Thomas J. Watson Jr., son of the legendary general manager, nearly one hundred years ago, and the company is exceptionally skilled at anticipating and actively shaping future trends (such as cloud computing) to fuel revenue growth. This all stems from an intensive coaching program for senior leaders, plus frequent rotation across businesses and geographies to build those competencies. Not surprisingly, IBM became a huge success story over this decade, outperforming many of its traditional competitors, such as HP.

These are corporate examples, but there's nothing preventing you, the individual leader, from being as disciplined about aligning your people-development practices with your situation and goals. Your aim should be to cultivate a balanced team and to build everyone's unique strengths to the highest levels of mastery.

# Capuchin Monkeys
# and Equal Pay

One of my favorite TED talks in recent years was by the prima-
tologist Frans de Waal. It includes a fabulous video clip of two
female capuchin monkeys in adjacent transparent cages, each giving pebbles to a researcher in exchange for small pieces of cucum-
ber.[1] They make this trade twenty-five times in a row until the
researcher starts giving one monkey a grape—a much better treat.
Immediately, the second monkey, who's still getting the cucum-
ber, becomes furious. She throws the food back, wrathfully bangs
the floor, and pounds at the cage. You see, even monkeys understand the difference between fair and unfair compensation.

When it comes to people—to attracting, retaining, and motivating them—pay is also important. Like those monkeys, humans
expect to be compensated for the labor they provide, in a way
that accurately reflects their contribution or effort and is com-
parable to what others doing similar jobs are paid. As one of my
engineering professors once told me, "It's amazing to see how

creative someone can become when he's confronted by a huge pile of dollars." And research by neuroscientists has indeed shown that financial incentives trigger one of the most primitive parts of the brain, the nucleus accumbens, or "pleasure center," which is also responsible for the "high" you get from drugs, sex, and gambling.[2] So we do like money, and we will perform to get it.

However, in my experience, while unfair pay can surely demotivate (as it did with those monkeys), compensation beyond that is way less important than most people think, especially among knowledge workers. At one point, I carefully looked into cases of candidates recommended by our firm who were successful in their new jobs but still left them within three years. I found that 85 percent were hired away into a more senior position, which confirms they were competent people with high potential. But when I inquired about the reasons for their departures, I discovered that only 4 percent cited money as the primary reason. More often their departures had been prompted by bad bosses, limited integration support, or lack of opportunities for further growth.

Similarly, when Jim Collins tried to determine the relationship between a company's executive compensation levels and systems and its ability to transition from "good to great," he concluded, after 112 analyses, that there was no pattern. Money wasn't nothing; great companies did pay slightly above average to stay competitive. But their real advantage was having people with an intrinsic motivation to deliver their best.[3]

In his excellent book *Drive*, Daniel H. Pink beautifully summarizes the history and essence of human motivation, highlighting the gap between what science knows and what business practices.[4] As he puts it, external, carrot-and-stick financial incentives were fine for routine twentieth-century tasks. But they are incompatible with how we work today. Now, we are driven by three essential things: (1) autonomy—the freedom to direct our lives; (2) mastery—the desire to achieve excellence in what we do; and (3) purpose—the knowledge that what we do is in service of something bigger than ourselves.

As a leader, you can emulate organizations like Google, which famously gives its employees "20 percent time" to focus on whatever they want, or Zappos, which doesn't monitor the call times of its customer service representatives or require them to use scripts. Offer your people autonomy along four "T" dimensions: task (what they do), time (when they do it), team (who they do it with), and technique (how they do it).

Also help them toward mastery not only with development opportunities but also by allowing and encouraging them to engage more fully in their work. This state of "flow" arises when you set difficult but attainable challenges and eliminate distractions so they can become immersed and work at maximum efficiency. Atos, an IT services company, is, for example, pursuing a zero e-mail policy to let its people focus on more important tasks.

Finally, point them to a greater cause. Unfortunately, traditional businesses have long considered purpose ornamental at best, a nice paragraph on their mission statements and annual reports. But as aging baby boomers confront their own mortality and idealistic youth demand more from their jobs, this won't be enough. Tell your people what good will come from their work, whether it's "every day low prices" at Walmart or to be "the fabric of real-time communication for the web" at Skype.

Do pay well too, ideally above average. But realize that money will never motivate the wrong people to do the right thing. Instead incentivize all the right people you've picked with the opportunity to play independent roles on your team, to master their skills, and to pursue broader team, organizational, or societal goals.

# Second Chances

Ricardo Garay, known by everyone for his last name as "Garay," is the gaucho we hired to manage our ranch in Patagonia back in 2000, right after we bought it. Short, fit, and slim, tough, alert, and hardworking, he came highly recommended by two people: a farm broker who had lived his whole life in the area and another local who helped us with the initial purchase and takeover of the property. This was an important decision. Our ranch sits in a part of Patagonia that is almost one thousand miles from our home in Buenos Aires, with no communication, so I needed someone I could trust. And Garay seemed to fit the bill. He would start every day before dawn and ride his horse up the Andes through the night, if needed, to check the place.

But not long after he started, problems arose. He was constantly fighting with our neighbors and external contractors who had to visit for special tasks. We tolerated this behavior for four years until one heated discussion about a visitor he would not receive. "I don't accept that person coming in," he told me. "If you want him to, you will need to fire me." So I did. At age forty-eight, it was the first time I'd ever let someone go. Over the following six years, we hired a series of successors and had terrible experiences with each. While the "stick rate" of Garay was four years, no one else lasted more than two, and we asked one gaucho to leave even before the end of the customary three-month trial period. Eventually, my wife, María, said: "Shouldn't we consider hiring back Garay? Why don't we meet with him, talk about what happened in the past, check whether we can agree on what needs to be done including how he handles contractors, and see whether it could make sense?" We did just that.

Garay came back and successfully helped us consolidate our incipient cattle-fattening operation for the next several years. Unfortunately for us, his personal circumstances eventually changed, and he left to be closer to his family in San Martín de los Andes, but we see him occasionally and miss him greatly.

So what lessons did I take from this experience of hiring back a man I'd fired? That sometimes people who you don't expect to grow or develop into stars deserve a second chance—or at least a second glance. And when you give it to them, keep three things in mind.

First, benchmark against the field of candidates. In Patagonia, the market for gaucho talent is tight. Only after interviewing dozens of them through the years and working with several failures, did we realize that Garay was probably one of the best in the area. Highly educated people with great social skills aren't typically willing to live alone in the remote mountains, riding a horse around for hours through frozen blizzards and heavy winds. Garay was, and he did it well.

Second, accept trade-offs. Garay's successors ranged from highly sophisticated newcomers to Patagonia who excelled at coordinating contractors and handling administrative tasks, to fully illiterate locals who truly loved the more physical aspects of the job. None did both well, and we realized that we couldn't expect Garay to either.

Third, recognize that timing and circumstances matter. The critical competencies for any job are dynamic. In the early years, when we had no cattle, our priority was to rapidly fix up the ranch, so external help was essential, as was a person who could tolerate, if not manage, it. But once the fencing, utility building, and grass-seeding were accomplished, different skills were required. With fewer people around the ranch and more cattle, we were vulnerable to poachers and furtive hunters; Garay's firm hand in dealing with strangers (and a healthy suspicion of anyone) was suddenly an asset. Not a single calf disappeared after his return.

How can you put this advice to work in more traditional and civilized environments? Make sure to get a feel for the universe of potential candidates; otherwise you can significantly underhire, or eternally search for a perfect person who doesn't exist. Once you've done that, realistically weigh the inevitable trade-offs, since you can't have it all. If you realize that no one person can do the essentials of the job, you might consider hiring multiple people with complementary skills or developing the candidate who comes the closest. And be aware of changing circumstances. Never assume that people who were great at yesterday's job will be good at today's.[1] And never assume that people who aren't stars today couldn't be tomorrow.

Every time I see Garay in San Martín de los Andes, I'm reminded of that.

# PART FIVE

# Teams That Thrive

The best get even better when they work together. As a leader, it's your job to build a diverse, effective, committed group capable of achieving collective greatness.

# Bringing Stars
# Together

In my early years as an executive search consultant, I was frequently asked to hire senior investment bankers. J.P. Morgan and Citibank were in those days the leading players in Argentina, but as I contacted and interviewed most of their key bankers, I saw something strange going on. While both had top people, one was dramatically more successful in the market. How did the stars at that firm manage to shine brightly together, while those at the other merely twinkled on their own? For years, I puzzled over the huge performance gaps I often saw between teams that, on paper, looked as if they would be equally effective. You see it in business, in sports, in creative endeavors from movies to magazines. What made the difference? And what was the secret to both evaluating and enhancing *team*, rather than individual or organizational, dynamics?

My questions were answered in the late 1990s when my great colleague Elaine Yew led a firmwide project called the Team Effectiveness

Review, or TER. This proprietary model analyzes six critical team competencies, summarized in figure 31-1.

The underlying premise is that it's not enough to just hire the right people—those with strong values, great potential, and high competence—and develop them as individuals. You also have to help them work together. Indeed, based on our firm's fifty years of practice and research, we believe that team effectiveness explains perhaps 80 percent of leaders' success.

Don't believe the popular myth that groups of all-stars don't work. Of course they do, if you structure and lead them properly. Bain & Company's Michael Mankins, Alan Bird, and James Root illustrate all sorts of wonderful examples in their *Harvard Business Review* article "Making Star Teams Out of Star Players."[1] Some are huge project teams, like the six hundred Apple engineers who

**FIGURE 31-1**

## Team Effectiveness Review

How well a team understands the importance of diversity of skills and strengths and is willing to incorporate them

How well a team understands the need to optimize resources and time and drives efficiently for results

How well team members understand the larger collective purpose, and focus their actions and those of the team on that objective

Balance
Efficiency
Alignment
Openness
Resilience
Energy

How much a team values engaging with the broader organization and the outside world and builds the connections to do so

How well a team can hold itself together, even under severe internal or external stress, and remain effective

How ambitious the team is, and how much it takes the initiative and maintains long-term momentum at a high level

Low  Medium  High

*Source:* Copyright Egon Zehnder.

successfully developed the revolutionary OS X operating system in just two years (compared with the five years it took ten thousand Microsoft engineers to develop, and eventually retract, Microsoft's Windows Vista). Others are small creative teams, such as the one that so successfully lead the development of the digitally animated marvel *Toy Story* (which included Pixar's top artists and animators, Disney's veteran executives, and Steve Jobs himself).

You can and should create an A-team. But remember that it will only thrive when you've made it balanced, aligned, resilient, energetic, open, and efficient. In fact, big weakness in any of those six competencies can lead to big problems, as figure 31-2, highlighting some classically dysfunctional teams, illustrates.

FIGURE 31-2

## Some classically dysfunctional teams

| Team is low in: | Description |
|---|---|
| Efficiency    Alignment<br> | **The debating society**<br>• Issues: Team lacks the ability to prioritize.<br>• What it looks like: Team tolerates too much complexity and can't make timely decisions; members thwart alignment by constantly presenting new arguments and refusing to accept trade-offs.<br>*"No one can agree on anything except that there's more to be said."*<br>• Impact: Team misses deadlines and fails to complete tasks. |
| Balance<br><br>Openness | **The overly tribal**<br>• Issues: Team is "inbred" and lacks diverse perspectives.<br>• What it looks like: Team agrees on everything, has a shared identity distinct from rest of organization, and makes decisions quickly because alternatives aren't really considered.<br>*"If it wasn't invented here, no one wants it—new ideas are shown the door."*<br>• Impact: Team clings to the status quo, resists change or integration with others, and misses opportunities. |
| <br>Resilience<br>Energy | **The victim of events**<br>• Issues: Team lacks the resources to resolve conflicts or recover from setbacks.<br>• What it looks like: Team feels beaten down and impotent or is fragmented; members lack the drive to act and blame others, or each other, for failures.<br>*"Everyone thinks the problem is too big to be fixed and things are out of their hands."*<br>• Impact: Team reacts slowly, wastes time pointing fingers, accomplishes little. |

*Source*: Copyright Egon Zehnder.

So rate your team on each of the TER dimensions, using psychometrics, questionnaires, and (most effective) interviews and references by objective assessors. Are you building enough diversity of skills and strengths? Is everyone aligned with your fundamental purpose? Are you all properly prepared to face the inevitable hard times? How ambitious is your team? Have you developed a wide array of internal and external networks? Are you optimizing the use of your time and resources?

Revisiting those teams of investment bankers, I realized that the winning firm had a group that was much more diverse in terms of skills and backgrounds. (In fact, one top player was a college dropout and still whole-heartedly embraced by his colleagues with business and finance degrees.) Members were incredibly aligned with each other and fully committed to the organization, making it almost impossible to hire anyone away, even at a huge premium in compensation. They were upbeat and engaged, open to new ideas, and able to bounce back from adversity. And, thanks to solid processes and protocols, they were able to collaborate efficiently and effectively.

As a leader, it's your job to ensure that the stars you've chosen shine not just alone but also in a beautiful constellation. If your TER scores are low, you have some serious work to do, which I'll address in chapter 32.

{ 32 }

# Fit for a Purpose

In October 2008, the US stock market was in free fall, having plummeted almost 30 percent over the previous five weeks. Credit markets were stagnant. Formerly iconic companies like Lehman Brothers had gone bankrupt. Houses in Las Vegas had lost 40 percent of their value. Hundreds of billions of dollars had been committed to failing financial firms. And confidence in the US government was the lowest pollsters had ever measured.

The major US banks and credit-ratings agencies were called before Congress to testify and publicly shamed. They had created, endorsed, and sold thousands of securities based on risky, subprime mortgages that were now in default or about to be. One agency had told investors that the default risk to its AAA-rated CDOs was only 0.12 percent over the next five years. In fact, the default rate turned out to be 28 percent, over two hundred times worse than predicted.[1] Executives were accused of everything from complete ignorance to gross negligence to profit-protecting collusion.

Just a few months later, a new president bravely took the reins of one of these financial institutions, determined to renew its integrity and professionalism and reinforce its mission of bolstering the global banking system. He inherited a team of executives with long tenures at the company (though few knew each other well) and then added some less seasoned people in whom he saw great potential. His next step was to agree to work with our firm on a Team Effectiveness Review (TER) to better understand the group he'd gathered around him and take it to the next level.

We found some positive signs but also several problems. In terms of *balance*, high diversity on the team was offset by low trust. People showed *alignment* in recognizing common objectives but they still focused primarily on their own priorities. *Resilience* was strong; everyone who'd survived the crisis had learned to perform under pressure. But there wasn't sufficient *energy* to meet the new president's ambitious goals. *Openness* was also lacking thanks to an inward-looking, consensus-oriented legacy culture. And *efficiency* was low, with effective targets and monitoring derailed by meetings not designed for decision making.

The president decided to address the biggest deficiencies—in openness and efficiency—first. He introduced new rules of engagement to encourage healthy debate, including drawing out each stakeholder's perspectives at executive committee meetings and pushing for new thinking from within and outside the company. He also worked hard to sort out more efficient business unit/ functional collaboration through protocols on how and when to include which people. Over time, the positive tone he set and improved team outcomes began to boost comfort levels between members. Today, the group is scoring much higher on all the TER measures, and that is filtering down into the rest of the firm. As I write this, the finance sector is still working to atone for its prior sins. But I have no doubt that, if there is another global financial crisis soon, this company won't be to blame.

Just as no executive will ever be perfect, neither will any team shine on all six TER dimensions. Your job is to make sure it's strong enough in each to meet your specific challenges. Different

FIGURE 32-1

## Different situations require different team patterns

| Challenge | Particular strengths required | Comments |
|---|---|---|
| **Turnaround** | Efficiency / Resilience | • Resilience: Turnarounds are high-pressure situations. The team needs to continue to function in the face of a challenging internal and external environment.<br>• Efficiency: Getting things done fast and keeping up momentum is crucial. |
| **New venture** | Openness / Resilience / Energy | • Openness: New ventures require staying particularly close to changes in the environment and continuous monitoring and adaptation.<br>• Resilience: New ventures are high-pressure situations. In this "forming" stage, there are inevitably some "collisions" between team members as they work to establish norms, arising from trial and error.<br>• Energy: All team members must be self-driving and feel full ownership for getting things done whether or not directly their formal responsibility. |
| **Post-merger integration** | Balance / Alignment | • Balance: Respecting and using the diversity of strengths and views of both sides of the merger.<br>• Alignment: The team must drive one clear joint mission on both sides and ensure clear and consistent communication at all times, speaking as one. |

*Source*: Copyright Egon Zehnder.

situations require different team patterns: For example, as figure 32-1 illustrates, turnaround teams need to be very strong in *efficiency* and *resilience,* while groups working on a postmerger integration need to excel at *balance* and *alignment.* I frequently use the framework to help private equity firms gauge how the executive teams of potential acquisition targets fit with the respective investment theses.

While building and developing your team, start by thinking about your particular scenario and exactly what you need to succeed. How crucial will it be for your team to stay properly balanced, aligned, resilient, energetic, open, or efficient? Once you have that clear, you can identify and address the largest gaps.

Make sure you also get the entire team to agree on collective priorities and group action items, as well as personal ones. My colleagues in Italy recently worked for one of the country's largest industrial companies on an interesting initiative that included an official "team deal" highlighting collective goals and guidelines for behavior; an "individual deal" requiring a pledge from each team member to participate; and a kit of "audit tools" allowing the team to monitor its progress. As a result, the group has indeed become best in class on all the TER performance dimensions.

{ 33 }

# From Counting People to Making People Count

I grew up in a Buenos Aires neighborhood full of people just like my family and me—middle-class Catholics of Caucasian descent. I went to a Catholic, all-boys high school and then studied industrial engineering for six years at the Argentine Catholic University without a single woman in my class. My first exposure to any form of cultural, gender, religion, racial, or class diversity was at Stanford's Graduate School of Business, where I got my MBA, and I loved it. I found an extremely open, international campus community and became quite intrigued with the various affirmative action initiatives I saw deployed at the school and in the United States more broadly. I was grateful for them, since my foreignness had certainly helped me get in and win a fellowship to Stanford and I knew that well-deserving classmates had reaped similar benefits. But I still wondered about the effectiveness of such programs.

Over the following three decades, I've watched many organizations experiment with ways of promoting women and minorities with mixed success and mixed impact on performance. So the question remains: *Does diversity really work and, if so, under what conditions?*

It's very hard to measure true diversity, which is about the variety of skills, strengths, and perspectives on a team. When looking at the most tangible dimensions, such as nationality (as a proxy for culture) and gender, the evidence suggests that a mix does boost organizational success. Recently, McKinsey mapped the earnings before interest and tax (EBIT) margins and return on equity (ROE) of 180 publicly traded companies in France, Germany, the United Kingdom, and the United States against the gender balance and spread of nationalities represented on their executives boards, and the results were quite conclusive: The ROE at companies in the top quartile for board diversity was 53 percent above that of those in the bottom quartile, while EBIT margins were 14 percent higher.[1] In Egon Zehnder's executive database, we also find that leadership teams high on the diversity competence also tend to be very strong in strategic orientation, commercial orientation, and change leadership. Simply put, diverse groups have great potential to add value because they see more and better possibilities, do more and better deals, and get the best out of each other.

Still, many people remain skeptical of diversity initiatives—and, indeed, there are countless stories about ones that have failed or backfired. The truth is that highly heterogeneous teams fall at *both* extremes of the performance distribution: they either do extremely well because they exploit the benefits, or they do quite poorly because they can't overcome the friction created when people with vast differences work together.[2] If you want to push your team into the former category, there are a few best practices to follow.

First, fight your biases against diversity. A good example comes from an experiment conducted with philharmonic orchestras hiring new musicians. When a screen was placed between the applicants and the judges during auditions, many more women were chosen.[3] The assessors were forced to focus on competence rather than subconsciously falling back on ingrained gender stereotypes, and so previously ignored talent was put to work, improving the quality and performance of the whole team. Always consider candidates from grossly underrepresented categories. You don't have to hire or promote them if they aren't future stars, but if you fail to consider any in the first place, you're virtually guaranteed to miss someone who could have improved your team.

Second, educate and train yourself and your team in how to exploit diversity. Here I'm talking about all kinds of differences, from gender to generation, socioeconomic class to culture, functional experience to personality type. Management thinkers have published reams of advice addressing all of these categories, but I'll mention just a few. For an intro to the varying contributions of baby boomers, Gen Xers, and millennials, try management thinker Tammy Erickson's work.[4] To better understand what people from different national and ethnic backgrounds bring to the table, start with Gert Hofstede's five dimensions, which I referenced in chapter 23.[5] And for an appreciation of personalities that don't match your own, consider the Myers-Briggs Type Indicator (MBTI), which measures people on four spectrums: Extrovert/Introvert, iNtuitive/Sensing, Thinking/Feeling and Judging/Perceiving. One of the most valuable development programs in which I've participated was a course that trained attendees to identify and value these style differences, then reap the benefits of complementarity while minimizing conflict. More than two decades later, the lessons still help me both personally (since my wife, María, is an ENFP, the exact opposite of me, an ISTJ) and professionally (in my wallet, for example, I carry a handy card listing how ten different influence tactics will work on each of the sixteen MBTI types).

Whichever research or model you use, I can't emphasize enough the value of teaching your team how to understand and leverage varied perspectives—stemming from any factor—in a productive way. (I'll talk more about gender in the next essay.) Everyone should know that you see it as a fundamental leadership skill and a top development priority. When my colleagues and I evaluate candidates, we use a diversity-and-inclusion competency scale with seven levels. Executives at the lower levels are merely *reactive,* just accepting the potential value of different cultures and points of view. Those with middle-range scores are able to act on that understanding by changing their own perspectives, working effectively with diverse peers, seeking out opposing views, and making managerial and business decisions better tailored to the sociocultural environments in which they operate. Finally, leaders with the highest ratings in this competency *proactively* put diversity to work for their organizations, facilitating interaction between various groups and cultures and to educate and inspire others.

Out of thousands of senior managers we've evaluated over the last decade (including CEOs, CFOs, and other top executives), only 10 percent were at the highest levels in terms of diversity and inclusion. This is therefore a unique opportunity for those visionary managers genuinely committed to move from counting people to making people count.

# The Female
# Opportunity

Hixonia Nyasulu is a black woman who grew up in Johannesburg, South Africa, under apartheid. The daughter of a deep gold-mining operator, she attended a Durban boarding school on scholarship, then progressed to the University of Zululand, graduating with degrees in social work and psychology. Venturing to the United States, she studied at the Arthur D. Little School of Management (now the Hult International Business School), then scored a graduate trainee spot at consumer goods giant Unilever in 1978. Six years later, at age twenty-eight, she founded her own marketing and research company, propelling herself into the growing ranks of standout African business leaders. She has since founded Ayavuna Women's Investments, a female-led investment firm, and served for a stint as deputy chairman of Nedbank. And, until recently, she was the chairwoman of Sasol, an energy and chemical group that is one of South Africa's largest and most prestigious companies, with tens of thousands of employees in some forty countries, and she sits on both Unilever's board of directors and JPMorgan Chase's advisory board. A delightful person, married with three sons, she has done all this without any political affiliation. It's humbling to see how much she has achieved from such a disadvantaged background.

Over the past few years, as I've traveled the world to speak with senior private and public leaders about talent issues, typically leading more than one hundred workshops, seminars, or events annually, I'm often asked where I see the most opportunity. My answer is never a country, it's a gender: women. I'm constantly amazed by the exceptional caliber of the female leaders I see today—from famous political and business names, such as German Chancellor Angela Merkel, IMF's Managing Director Christine Lagarde, PepsiCo's CEO Indra Nooyi, and Facebook's COO Sheryl Sandberg, to lesser known ones whose careers I've tracked, such as Hixonia Nyasulu.[1] At the same time, I'm dismayed by the persistent dearth of women in the top echelons of companies. Even in the United States, a country that has made extraordinary progress since 1776, women only represent 15 percent of *Fortune* 500 executive officers and a mere 4 percent of CEOs, even though they account for 46.6 percent of the labor force and 51.4 percent of people in managerial, professional, and related occupations. Globally, executive committees of sizable companies are only 9 percent female, and women CEOs account for a token 2 percent of the total pool.[2] Given the escalating war for talent (driven by the unprecedented combination of globalization, demographics, and depleting pipelines of qualified leaders I described in chapter 7), a commitment to find, develop, and promote the best women seems like not only an obvious solution but also a historic opportunity.

And this is especially true in emerging markets. The BRIC markets (Brazil, Russia, India, and China) alone represent 40 percent of the world's population and have accounted for 45 percent of the world's growth since 2007, and women have played a big part in that success. They outperform men in both educational attainment (60 percent of college graduates in Brazil and 65 percent in

China are female) and ambition (with more than 70 percent in India, Brazil and China aspiring to top jobs). China has an amazing 75 percent female labor force participation; while in India and Brazil women respectively account for 11 percent and 12 percent of the CEOs leading top companies, more than five times the global average.[3]

What should you, an individual manager, do about this opportunity?

First, if you're a man, try to better understand the female perspective. Louann Brizendine's excellent small books *The Female Brain* and *The Male Brain* are a great place to start learning about the differences that generate so much complementary power when properly leveraged.[4] (Women will find these books equally useful!)

Also recognize that women are often unconsciously programmed to undervalue their potential, limit their goals and, as Sheryl Sandberg so put it, lean back instead of in.[5] You need to make sure your female employees don't fall into this trap. Scores of studies show the paradox that women face: many fail to advance because they don't promote their own interests, and yet those who do are held back too because they're perceived as aggressive, uncooperative, and selfish.[6] Until that situation changes, women will need strong sponsors, with real clout, to help them gain access to the development opportunities they deserve.[7]

Consider also flexible work arrangements that make it easier for the best women—including those committed to home and community responsibilities—to work for you. Potential offerings include extended maternity leaves, temporary part-time arrangements, remote work (provided there's still adequate time for in-person collaboration with the rest of the team), and flexible office hours. Men increasingly want these kinds of accommodations too. Make sure to carefully understand individual needs and cultural norms, however. For example, in some emerging markets, elder care is more of an issue than child care, and you should adjust your policies accordingly.

Last but certainly not least, if you're a senior leader responsible for organization-wide hiring decisions, consider imposing modest, temporary quotas at certain management tiers. In 2012, Italy enacted a law requiring that all publicly listed or state-controlled companies appoint people from an "underrepresented gender" to make up one-fifth of their boards (the quota will eventually rise to one-third).[8] There was strong resistance when the proposal was being debated but, once it passed, the reaction was, "If we need to bring on more women, let's at least get good ones." Candidate pools were broadened and more rigorous competency-based assessments applied. And most Italians agree that their boards are today much stronger as a result. The initial nudge seems to have brought unexpected benefits: having been made more aware of the quality of the women among them, Italians elected many more of them to Parliament in February 2013 elections. The country's governing body now boasts one of the world's largest female representations at about 32 percent, up from 21 percent before the elections.

# { 35 }

# A Culture of
# Unconditional Love

During my first decade in Egon Zehnder's Buenos Aires office, our
Argentine practice soared, recording the highest per capita financial
performance in the whole firm for five consecutive years in the late
1990s. But we all know what happened in 2001. By the end of the
year, Argentina's economy had collapsed. It was the largest sover-
eign debt default in world history, and GDP fell by some 30 percent
coupled with a 300 percent currency devaluation. Over twelve days,
five different presidents took control of the country. One bank lost
more money in a few weeks than it had accumulated over the previous century. There were companies with losses larger than their
sales, and in one memorable month, the number of new cars sold in
the country was lower than the number of cars stolen! As you can
imagine, that was not an easy time for me. No one in his right mind
was looking to hire an executive search consultant.

As that dramatic disintegration played out in early 2002, I had
to present our office's results and perspectives at the firm's annual

partners' meeting in Switzerland. As soon I walked on stage, the audience of some two hundred colleagues went dead silent, waiting to hear what I would say. I was solemn and candid. I told them that our brilliant past in Argentina would never be replicated; that I was expecting big losses and didn't see much future for our firm in the country. I said I would wait a year or so and then tell them very frankly whether it made any sense to stay.

As soon as I finished, one of our Dutch partners, Sikko Onnes, stood up and said, "Claudio, if I understand what you are implying, you are totally wrong. Our partnership has benefited from the extraordinary contribution of your office for well over a decade. Now it's the time for *us* to support *you*. Your only job is to go back to the Buenos Aires office and tell every single member of the consulting and support staff that they all have our full and unconditional support."

The whole group then stood up and applauded. I tried to thank Sikko, but I couldn't because I was in tears. What I felt then from my colleagues was unconditional love.

Thanks to our corporate culture, that love is something I get at work every single day and it's what encourages me to give my absolute best in return, for twenty-eight years now. Anyone who wants to not only select the best but also pull them together into a strong and lasting team can't do so without fostering a compelling and inspiring culture. That's how you overcome challenges and keep your mission going in your absence.

All serious research, all respected business thinkers, and all great leaders confirm this point. As Peter Drucker put it, "Culture eats strategy for breakfast." Just take a look at Southwest Airlines, the company that saw the greatest value expansion in the S&P 500 between 1971 and 2001. Herb Kelleher—its CEO for thirty-five years—once said: "Given enough time and money, your competitors can duplicate almost everything you've got working for you. They can hire away some of your best people. They can reverse-engineer your processes. The only thing they can't duplicate is your culture . . . Do you know the difference between strategy and culture? Well, when Napoleon was in Paris in a room with all his generals around a table, discussing how to attack Russia, that's strategy. But what makes 1,000,000 men march to Moscow, that is culture!"[1]

Even if you do everything I've advised in previous essays—hiring outstanding performers with great potential; appointing them to the right roles; identifying, retaining, motivating, and developing your brightest stars; building great teams fit for the purpose—you can't make the mistake of ignoring culture. If you do, you'll achieve very little, and it won't last long. Your people won't go as far as they could, or they will leave.[2]

So, how do you build a great culture? It starts with you, the leader, using it as a filter for hiring. My model is Egon Zehnder himself, who founded our firm and gave it his name. From the beginning, he vowed to consider only the strongest candidates to join him: people with double degrees from top schools, international experience, high emotional intelligence, and remarkable career trajectories. More important, he would never, ever, hire anyone who was not dying to work in a highly professional, ethical, collaborative firm. Before I joined, I was interviewed by some thirty-five partners, including all executive committee members, in five different countries, over a single week. Egon personally checked my references with McKinsey, my employer then. That's the standard process, and it remains intact today.[3] Until he retired as CEO, Egon met with and approved every single consultant who joined any of our sixty-eight offices around the world—for thirty-six years. Today, his successor, Damien O'Brien, continues the practice, no exceptions allowed.

The second step in building a culture is compassionate coaching. Once we're adults, our personal growth comes mostly from exposure to the complex challenges discussed in chapter 27 and from great developmental relationships—with bosses, mentors, and colleagues who engage us, motivate us, inspire us, and help us succeed. Great leaders are great listeners who make their employees feel valued, see the bigger picture, and feel a part of something important. Fascinating recent studies using fMRI (functional magnetic resonance imaging) to track neural activity show how that sort of coaching arouses the parasympathetic nervous system, invoking cognitive, emotional, perceptual, and behavioral openness and improving performance. It also creates the conditions for neurogenesis, allowing people to learn and develop new healthy habits and competencies. By contrast, coaching that focuses on weaknesses arouses the sympathetic nervous system and does just the opposite.[4] Compassionate coaches are not just positive cheerleaders but also committed guides, conscious of the state and progress of their team and the individuals in it. They are also timely provocateurs, offering the right dose of tough love when necessary.

These hiring and coaching practices demand extraordinary discipline. But it's worth it to create a culture of unconditional love that perpetuates itself and binds your team together into a whole bigger than the sum of its parts.

{ 36 }

# Lone Wolves
# Starving

As a member of Egon Zehnder's global executive committee, I've thought a great deal about how to compensate our partners. The best advice I ever received on the matter came from a Harvard Business School program called Leadership in Professional Service Firms. I took it in early 2000. At that time, our firm was doing very well, but I was nonetheless concerned about the imminent retirement of our founder, the rise of the internet in the search profession, and the fact that some of our major competitors had recently gone public and begun to pursue aggressive global expansion.

In one of the sessions, the professor, Ashish Nanda, explained that there were two basic compensation models in firms such as ours. The prevalent one is *eat-what-you-kill*, in which people's pay directly reflects the business they generate and the work they produce for clients. This seems equitable and economically logical. The second model is the *lockstep*, in which people's pay is unrelated to their personal contribution and instead varies according to some preestablished formula related to years of service, years as a part-ner, or participation in local or global profits. On the surface, in capitalist cultures at least, this seems to make less sense: shouldn't a lawyer or consultant's pay reflect the value that person adds?

At that point, Nanda asked how many people in the class were paid in a lockstep system. Out of eighty students, only eight, including me, raised their hands. He then asked how many of us were from Ameri-can firms, and everyone put their hands down. The lockstep was a very rare species, almost nonexistent in the United States. That gave me an additional reason to worry: were we doing something wrong?

To my relief, Nanda surprised us with his follow-up. He told us that while most professional service firms follow an eat-what-you-kill sys-tem, in nearly every sector there are a few locksteps—which tend to have the best reputation, the highest profitability, and the nicest cul-ture. He mentioned the law firm Wachtell, Lipton, Rosen & Katz, as well as McKinsey. The key to outdoing the eat-what-you-kill model, he explained, was rigorous people processes and strong culture.

First, let's consider how compensation would work in typical lock-step and eat-what-you-kill systems that don't meet those two basic conditions. In figure 36-1, the diagonal line represents the eat-what-you-kill scenario: professional C produces nothing and gets nothing; professional A is a star and gets the highest pay; and professional B is an average producer who gets an average pay. The horizontal line represents a pure lockstep, where all those professionals earn exactly the same amount regardless of how much they contribute. What do you expect to happen in the latter case? Your star A would rail against being paid the same as lazy C and leave to make twice as much money at an eat-what-you-kill firm. C would never leave, since he gets a free ride, compared with nothing at an eat-what-you-kill firm. B would be constantly weighing her options: work more and switch teams; work less and stay. With this formula, the lockstep firm will lose all its stars and get stuck with the losers.

But great people practices can help to overcome this problem as illustrated in figure 36-2. If you weed out all the Cs—mainly

FIGURE 36-1

## Eat-what-you-kill versus lockstep

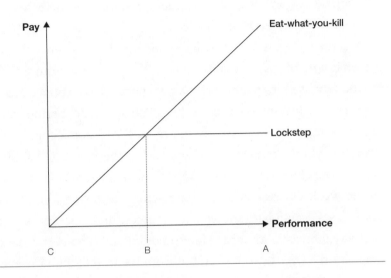

FIGURE 36-2

## Great hiring in locksteps

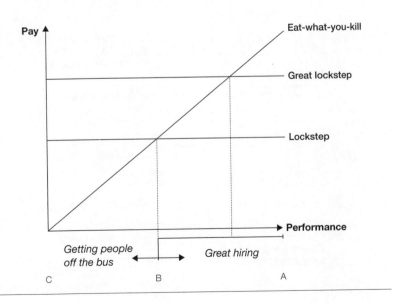

through great hiring but also by periodically reviewing existing employees and, if necessary, getting rid of the weakest—you're left with all A's and B's, your average performance increases and you're able to pay everyone more.

Of course, there's still a threat of your stars leaving, since the top eat-what-you-kill pay remains higher. That's where culture kicks in: you have to hire people with a penchant for collaboration and then constantly reinforce those values. When you do, performance increases again, as illustrated in figure 36-3. At Egon Zehnder, for example, where compensation depends on the firm's global profits, our consultants are always happy to have the best-qualified colleague work on assignments.[1] Rather than hoarding, they freely share cases, candidate knowledge, sources, and references. Productivity increases, as does value to our clients. The performance range is no longer from B to A, but from B+ to A+, with the average pay coming in at an even higher level.

FIGURE 36-3

**Strong culture in locksteps**

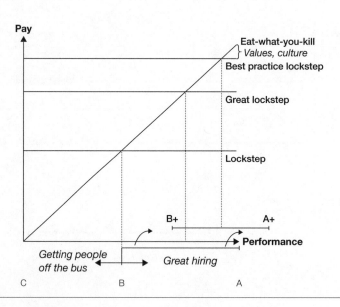

Yes, your superstar A could perhaps still make a bit more money in an eat-what-you-kill. But she will realize that her performance might suffer when her collaborative colleagues are replaced by more competitive, self-interested ones. If she instinctively values teamwork, or has learned to do so, she'd also feel out of place and desperately miss the camaraderie that comes with a professional family. Why be a lone wolf starving when you can hunt with others and feast together?

In today's knowledge economy, value comes from collectively creating and seamlessly sharing information.[2] When leading a team of any size, do whatever is in your power to make sure the incentives for meeting collective goals outweigh those for individual performance. Then adopt the kind of people practices and culture that will keep the strongest wolves in your pack.

{ 37 }

# It's All in the Family

One of the most memorable business meetings I've ever had was with the executive chairman of a successful family business. He told me he had a personal matter to discuss and invited me to his apartment in La Isla, one of the nicest neighborhoods in Buenos Aires. His kind and elegant wife greeted me at the door, showed me to a seat near her husband, served us tea, and then discreetly vanished. I sensed that something special was happening.

The man, who was in his seventies, leaned forward and spoke in a calm voice that carried a clear emotional undercurrent. "Listen, Mr. Fernández-Aráoz," he said, "I will get straight to the point. I have a bad cancer and my days are numbered. I run a family company, now in its third generation, and I want to ask you whether my son, Alberto, is the best CEO to take over when I die. I've asked you to come to my home and meet me in person because I want to look into your eyes when you answer. I don't want compassion. I want the best for my company and my family, long after I'm gone, and so I beg you for your most professional and honest reply."

I knew the company and Alberto very well, and was relieved to report that he was indeed fully qualified. A short time later, the man succumbed to his illness and his son took over, ushering in an outstanding period of growth, profitability, professionalization, and diversification that would have made his father immensely proud. Eventually, after some seven years as CEO, Alberto called me himself to say he thought the time had come for him to find his own successor. He was about to turn fifty and was no longer motivated to perform at such a high level in such a demanding executive role. This time, there were no internal candidates or family members qualified. Over the following years, we helped hire two outsiders to assume his responsibilities. The company, which recently celebrated its hundred-year anniversary, is now enjoying record performance, outpacing both its sector and the Argentine market.

This story illustrates both the dramas and challenges of family businesses and the best practices for propelling them into lasting greatness.

Family businesses play a huge role in the global economy. The term might call to mind small mom-and-pop shops, but thousands of organizations (including Ford, Fiat, BMW, Porsche, Peugeot, and Toyota, just to focus on the auto industry) are all still influenced or controlled by the families that founded them. Indeed, I've just described 30 percent of large companies in the United States and Europe, and more than 60 percent of those in East Asia and Latin America. There are benefits to keeping business in the family, or keeping families in the business. Research has shown that such organizations have a longer-term perspective, are much more prudent in terms of financial leverage and, according to McKinsey, generate total shareholder returns that outperform the MSCI World, S&P 500, and MSCI Europe indices by two to three percentage points across most geographies and industries.[1]

But the downsides cannot be ignored. Family businesses can struggle with leadership transitions, and there is often nepotism or infighting over the distribution of money and power. It's very hard to be objective about your relatives, especially your children. Even the gender of eldest children can affect decision making at the top in family businesses. A study with a unique data set from Denmark found that when a departing CEO has a firstborn daughter, a family successor is appointed in 29.4 percent of cases but when the firstborn is a son, that figure rises to 39 percent.[2] Unfortunately, global research has shown that family CEO successions dramatically reduce firm profitability (by at least four percentage points), putting many of these companies into the red, while relatively less-profitable firms led by family CEOs are more likely than professionally run firms to file for bankruptcy or be liquidated.

So how do you navigate this balance, keeping the best aspects of family businesses while avoiding the pitfalls? By implementing three best practices I've seen employed by successful, long-lasting family-controlled or family-influenced companies all over the world: strong boards, meritocracy, and disciplined leadership transitions.

You need fresh strategic perspectives from qualified outsiders to complement the family's skills and knowledge, so make sure you have a significant number of truly independent directors on your board. Corporate governance practices of most great family companies actually surpass those of your typical public company.

Clearly defined, uncompromising standards of meritocracy will also help you override the very natural human desire to favor your own kin. Many strong family companies decide that none of their members should be involved in management at all; others welcome family participation but require everyone to first successfully work outside the business for some time, or to diligently work their way from the bottom up inside, with their performance and career prospects evaluated every year by competent outsiders reporting to the board. All three approaches work as long as they're adhered to with discipline.

Finally, you must recognize that CEO succession is your toughest challenge and address it proactively and strategically. The best-run family businesses start planning these transitions years in advance. An independent board member, often advised by qualified professional consultants, leads a thorough review of the alignment and potential conflicts between family, owners, and managers and builds a consensus among all key stakeholders on the ideal profile of successor. The group then identifies, investigates, and evaluates candidates, being clear about the challenges the role presents. Once chosen, the new CEO—insider or outsider—goes through a formal integration process so the handover goes as smoothly as possible.

Great family companies have beautifully prospered for generations by following these rules. You might be able to find and develop the best among your sisters and brothers, sons and daughters, nephews and nieces. Or you might not. An independent board, a clear meritocracy, and careful attention to CEO succession will help guide your decisions.

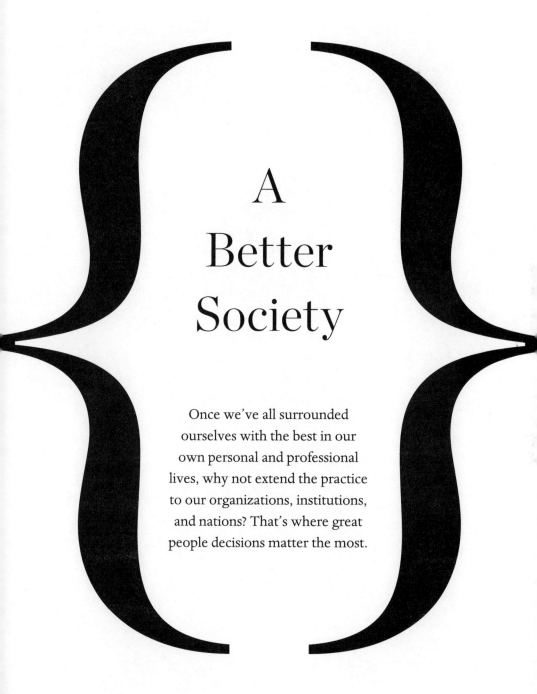

PART SIX

# A
# Better
# Society

Once we've all surrounded
ourselves with the best in our
own personal and professional
lives, why not extend the practice
to our organizations, institutions,
and nations? That's where great
people decisions matter the most.

{ 38 }

# Russian Roulette
# at the Top

Until now, all the stories I've told and advice I've given in this book have been directed at you, the individual manager, who wants to hire the best people possible and help them to further excel. But I would also like to improve the collective people decisions we all make in our organizations and societies. It's hard for you to be a good manager without support from your own boss; she can't be a good one without help from hers; and so on up the line all the way to the CEO.

As I mentioned before, there are huge differences in the outcomes generated by the best and worst corporate leaders. In the Morten T. Hansen, Herminia Ibarra, and Urs Peyer analysis that identified Jeff Bezos and Roger Agnelli as two of the top four CEO value creators in the world (along with Steve Jobs and Yun Jong-Yong), there was a dramatic contrast. Of the more than three thousand large-company chief executives they evaluated, the top one hundred delivered a total shareholder return of 1,385 percent during their tenures, while the bottom hundred presided over a collective decline of –57 percent, destroying more than half the value they had received. Organizations that choose the *right* CEO create prosperity not only for their investors but also for their employees and customers.[1]

Unfortunately, many fail to do so—with disastrous consequences. In *How the Mighty Fall*, Jim Collins analyzes the reasons for the decline of several previously great companies. In all but one case, CEO succession was to blame, whether it was a domineering leader staying on too long; an able executive dying or departing with no good replacement; talented internal candidates turning down the top job or unexpectedly leaving; a board of directors acrimoniously divided; a family business operating like a monarchy; or an outsider not embracing the company's core values.[2] Businesses built over decades can be rapidly destroyed with just one wrong appointment.

Of course, these transitions are extremely difficult for organizations for a few reasons. First, the people making the decisions—typically board members—tend to have very limited experience doing so: according to our studies, most have participated in no previous succession, or just in one. Second, the pool of candidates also lack previous similar experience: our research shows that more than 80 percent of newly appointed CEOs have never served in a chief executive role before. That will always be the case unless you want the same old executives rotating through top jobs at different companies. But such transitions are often a problem because the move from even a C-level job to CEO cannot be compared with any other career transition: you no longer have a day-to-day boss or any peers; you're the final decision maker on a huge variety of complex issues; and you face enormous exposure. What happens when inexperienced selectors are choosing from inexperienced candidates? Russian roulette at the top. It's a huge risk, with the wrong CEO potentially becoming a deadly bullet right at the organization's head.

Given the huge stakes, what are the best practices for CEO succession? First, start planning *very* early, ideally when the new CEO takes charge, but never later than three to four years before he or she expects to leave.

Second, create and maintain a clear outline of what you need from the CEO role, informed by the board and detailing all the required competencies, then regularly assess your leader against it. This might seem hard to do, but if you do it at lower levels, shouldn't you also do it at the top where it matters the most?

Third, build your internal bench identifying, assessing, and developing potential CEO candidates and benchmarking them against the best external talent.

Fourth, look externally for more candidates, ideally periodically but certainly as a planned succession approaches or following an unexpected departure. As I detailed in chapter 4, it's critically important to consider both insiders and outsiders, particularly for this role. Executive search firms can add great value here, but make sure to avoid or at least be aware of contingency arrangements or percentage fees that often cause them to favor external appointments over internal ones.

Fifth, require the board to conduct periodic emergency succession drills, since about 50 percent of CEO successions are unplanned.[3]

Finally, in this case more than ever, have a robust transition process, as I described in chapter 24. Studies show, for example, that outsiders who join the company three to four years before they become CEOs do just as well as insiders with much longer tenures.[4]

It's a long and challenging list. But given what's at stake, no organization should play Russian roulette when choosing its CEO. Check the barrel and put your company out of harm's way.

{39}

# True Leading Boards

Each person working in your organization plays a role in its success. But you can't succeed without the right people at the very top, and that includes not just the C-suite but also every member of the board. I was recently asked to consult a very delicate assignment for a major global corporation. The CEO left unexpectedly, and the board didn't see any obvious internal successors. My colleagues and I rapidly put together a list of external candidates while also insisting on appraising the best internal ones. However, during the latter process, we discovered something alarming: the company had no clear strategy, and the board was far from aligned on critical issues—including whether to take an important part of the organization public, pursue a big takeover/merger, or make smaller, more targeted acquisitions. Although willing and able to recommend which executives would be the best fit for each of those alternatives, we also clearly told the directors that their dysfunction was putting the company at huge risk.

The situation reminded me of a much more dramatic case of corporate board ineptitude: Enron. Last year, I met a man who'd been a director at the bankrupt energy, commodities, and services group when its massive accounting fraud came to light. When I asked what had happened, he answered that too many board members were independent, and blamed their lack of inside knowledge of the company. Based on my experience advising board selection processes, I didn't buy it. In my view, the *right* independent directors would have stayed close enough to Enron's executives to uncover their wrongdoing. As Jeffrey Sonnenfeld put it in his brilliant 2002 *Harvard Business Review* article following those scandals, "What Makes Great Boards Great," "It's not rules or regulations. It's the way people work together."[1]

In the same way I think women represent a big, unexploited talent opportunity at the individual level, I would argue that great boards are underutilized at the team level.[2] With the right people on them, these groups can and should move from a purely compliance and certification purpose, important as that is, to true leadership, adding real value to companies through their vision and judgment.[3]

How do organizations get the right people on their boards? As in any executive search, you should create a profile of the ideal candidate but avoid the common bias toward the usual, narrow parameters that can only be met by a CEO or COO. You don't need everyone to have line experience at the highest level and exposure to your industry; you need exceptional proven competence in key areas that other board members don't have. Contrary to what the former Enron director said, you'll want a healthy mix of insiders, who provide critical company knowledge to the board, and outsiders, who offer different perspectives. Remember also to leverage cultural and gender diversity; as for any effective team, balance is critical.[4]

Board candidates should also be formally assessed not just on experience and cultural fit, but also on four specific board competencies. Two are related to judgment: *results orientation* (a strong focus on long-term value and a willingness to challenge the status quo) and *strategic orientation* (an ability to help shape and implement corporate strategy by raising key issues and providing relevant advice and counsel). The other two reflect values and behavior: *collaboration and influencing* (an openness to teamwork and robust, rigorous debate) and *integrity and independence* (a desire to take principled action, even at personal risk, for the good of the company).

You might also start to develop a "track" for great future board members within your company. Identify exceptional executive talent earlier and provide them with development opportunities including international and general management assignments and recommendations to sit on the boards of other organizations.

If you don't have the power to influence such high-level corporate decisions, take a grassroots approach. Prep yourself and your best people to be great directors by taking on work that either involves macro strategy and other broad issues or deepens knowledge in critical areas for boards in particular industries, such as risk management in financial services, or digital marketing in consumer products. Find internal sponsors, network externally, and aim appropriately, so you're lobbying for or pushing your people toward only those board spots that promote their professional growth.

In the United States alone, there are more than 12,000 public companies offering more than 100,000 opportunities for board service. Let's all work to get the best people on them.

# Thriving on Crises

The late 1940s were a tough time for Hewlett-Packard, the fledgling electronic equipment maker that would eventually become one of America's best-known technology companies. World War II had left business slow and finances strained. But as legions of great engineers streamed out of closing or soon-to-close US military labs, HP's legendary founders Bill Hewlett and Dave Packard realized they couldn't let such an amazing hiring opportunity pass them by. When asked how they could afford to keep taking on new people, their answer was simple: "How could we afford *not* to!" Years later, when asked about the biggest contributor to HP's success over the years, they routinely cited their willingness to invest in talent, no matter the external economic climate.

A similar story comes from Egon Zehnder in the early 2000s, which were bleak years for the executive search industry. First, the dot-com bubble burst, and the war for talent died. Billings plummeted and profit margins shrank dramatically. Then came the September 11 attacks, followed by full-fledged economic crises in the United States and Europe, the SARS scare in Asia, and war, with all its attendant uncertainties, first in Afghanistan, then in Iraq. Yet, our firm emerged stronger than ever because of the way we reacted. While most of our competitors dismissed up to 50 percent of their staffs, we barely downsized. We continued to hire outstanding consultants and elected every single candidate who came up for partner during that period. When the market recovered, we had an extraordinary team bound together in a dense social fabric. Having started the downturn at about half the size of our largest competitor, we were nearly equal by its end, growing 150 percent over six years, doubling our billings per consultant, and significantly boosting our profits. Other firms suffered significant financial losses, but we never lost a cent.[1]

As these stories show, the secret to successfully weathering any storm is to keep your long-term perspective. While most people become shortsighted and irrational during difficult times, visionary leaders and organizations stay calm and use them to their advantage, sprinting away from their competitors and never looking back.

Harvard Business School's Ranjay Gulati, Nitin Nohria, and Franz Wohlgezogen considered this phenomenon in an analysis of forty-seven hundred companies across three recessions, discovering that 9 percent were able to come out in much better positions than they entered. What united the winners was a "progressive" focus. They were extremely selective about when and where to cut and remained on the lookout for investment opportunities. Rather than thinking in *either/or* terms—you're either hiring or you're downsizing—they, like HP and our firm, embraced the *and*, understanding they could do both things if they were smart about it.[2]

The losers in crises are typically the ones that fire excessively, or wrongly. In its 2008 CEO succession study, Booz & Company found that companies in the sectors hardest hit by that year's global financial crisis had an outsized (that is, irrational) increase in leadership turnover: In financial services, it was 159 percent higher than the historical average; in energy, which suffered from enormous oil price volatility, 107 percent higher.[3] Some of this firing was perfectly warranted, since the competencies needed for many CEOs had changed. But a lot of those decisions were either too late (finally getting rid of a CEO who had never been qualified) or not justified (blaming the person rather than the circumstances, or what social psychologists call the *fundamental attribution error*). Boards and executives were taking action to show they were doing *something,* instead of pausing to consider what *the right thing* might be.

Another, perhaps more pervasive, error companies make during crises is to freeze hiring. During the most recent recession, The Boston Consulting Group and the European Association for People Management surveyed thirty-four hundred executives, including ninety senior human resources leaders, in more than thirty countries, to see how they were responding. The most frequent action (or reaction) was to scale back recruiting. At the same time, survey participants rated the selective hiring of high-performing employees from competitors as one of the three most effective responses to the *previous* crisis (from a list of twenty-two) and the one with the best impact on employee commitment.[4] This irrationality is widespread. Those who stay rational can take advantage of it.

In addition to being an extraordinary organizational opportunity, crises can also be a *personal* blessing in disguise because, if you react to them with a positive approach, you will come out a better leader. When famed management thinkers Warren G. Bennis and Robert J. Thomas conducted their well-known "geeks and geezers" research at the start of the new millennium—analyzing the differences between leaders born in or before 1925 and those born in or after 1970—they were struck by one unexpected common indicator of success. The best leaders in both eras had all endured tough experiences—*crucibles*—that inspired them, shaped them, and taught them how to lead. They had the ability to find meaning in and learn from even the most trying circumstances, and it was one of their greatest assets.[5]

Anytime you're struggling through a dark period, remember that the sun will shine again. Bless your crucibles. Stay calm, and don't lose your long-term perspective. Think twice before firing anyone. And master the magic of *and*, selectively investing in talent even if you have to downsize elsewhere at the same time. Sooner than you expect, the crisis will end and you will be thriving.

# Sustainability—the Virtuous Circle

I'll never forget a speech I heard Carlo De Benedetti, the former CEO and president of the Italian telecommunications company Olivetti, give in 1989. With absolute conviction, he told us that technology was about to kill communism. Now that someone in the Soviet Union could listen to the BBC with a small transistor radio and launch a small clandestine press using just a personal computer and a small printer, the country's leaders could no longer control the news, and people would mobilize toward a better order. Of course, his prophecy quickly came true, with revolutions in Poland, Hungary, East Germany, Bulgaria, Czechoslovakia, and Romania; the dismantling of the Berlin Wall and German reunification; the dissolution of the Soviet Union; the end of the Cold War; and the adoption of electoral democracy in about half of the countries of the world (at least officially) by the early 1990s.

Today, technology is ushering in a new wave of real-time, radical transparency, and what I expect it to kill is governments and businesses that persist in unsustainable, socially irresponsible practices, which hurt workers, communities, the environment, and ultimately the organizations themselves. As Michael Porter of Harvard Business School and Mark Kramer of the social impact advisory firm FSG, have argued, companies today should aim to create "shared value"—building economic value in a way that *also* produces value for society by addressing its problems. The best leaders are already ahead of this trend and surrounding themselves with other managers and employees keen to join them in the mission. But success depends on having the right sustainability leaders at the right time.

Christoph Lueneburger, author of *A Culture of Purpose* and founder of our firm's sustainability practice, has over the years worked with me and other colleagues on scores of searches for chief sustainability officers across all major industries, as well as for CEOs and board directors who see the issue as a strategic imperative.[1] From this experience, we've realized that companies need different types of people leading the charge, depending on where they stand. In the early stages, the mandate is to create a vision of sustainability, which demands executives with strong change leadership and influencing skills. To translate that vision into action successfully *and* profitably, managers need exceptional results and commercial orientation. Once that transformation is complete, there should be a progression to proactive sustainability, so leaders need outstanding strategic and commercial orientation to anticipate future needs and drive innovation and long-term relationships.[2]

The good news is that, although the global talent pool is shrinking, it's increasingly being filled by young, demanding, mobile knowledge workers interested in rising through the ranks to do these jobs. Millennials, born from the late 1980s to the early 2000s, will soon be the largest employee group in the history of the United States, more than 70 million strong, and represent an even larger proportion of the global population. They care deeply about sustainability, and the best of them will opt to work only for those companies that do too.

Take Patagonia, the world-famous apparel manufacturer. Its products are highly prized and highly priced, but the company values social responsibility over growth and attracts top-notch talent as a result. Founder Yvon Chouinard threw down the gauntlet a few years ago in a meeting about the winter catalogue. "These are beautiful pictures," he told his design team, "but how can we make sure that we *don't* sell people more stuff they don't need?" Patagonia soon took out a full-page ad in the *New York Times*, showing its best-selling product (a light down jacket) with a single line of text underneath: "Don't buy this jacket." This announced to customers that the company didn't want to add to the world's pollution and waste by selling a new version of the same product every year; it wanted to create high-value, long-lasting items as sustainably as possible. Since then, it has launched the Sustainable Apparel Coalition, roping in industry gorillas such as Nike, and has entered into a partnership with eBay to allow people to more easily find used Patagonia items.

When my colleague Christoph asked Chouinard about his talent strategy a few years ago, he explained that he'd once brought in an industrial psychologist to assess his team. The expert's conclusion? "These people are really unemployable anywhere else." What he meant was that Patagonia's managers choose to work for the company because they love its values and the sense of empowerment they get from their jobs. "The trick," Chouinard told Christoph, "is to hire great people and leave them alone." Patagonia's employees and executives feel good about making reliable products and encouraging responsible consumption. There's nowhere else they'd rather be, and perhaps, after working in such a purpose-driven place, anywhere else would seem intolerable.

Sustainability becomes a virtuous circle. When you pursue it, you get the smartest, most creative, passionate, and principled people to want to work for you. Then they help propel your company into the future, creating shared value for all.

# Electing Country Presidents

Every four years, the citizens of the United States make the world's most important "who" decision. They choose their president, putting him (or her) in charge of the largest economy and strongest military power on earth. This is a great responsibility. And yet the process by which politicians come to power—not just in the United States but everywhere—has huge room for improvement.

As you now know, great people decisions first start with a wide pool of candidates, including both insiders and outsiders. But around the globe, politics remains a dynastic business, populated by familiar names such as Kennedy, Clinton, and Bush in the United States; Gandhi in India; and Aquino in the Philippines. Yes, Barack Obama, a mixed-race "outsider," won the US election in 2008. But had Hillary Clinton beat him for the Democratic Party nomination in 2008, as she nearly did, then won the general election against John McCain, the United States would have been led by two families, represented by a father and a son and a husband

and a wife, for twenty-four years, almost a quarter of a century. Even in a medium-sized family company, that type of leadership succession would not be taken seriously. Yet it almost happened in a nation of 300 million people. (And, as I write, Hillary Clinton is at 2/1 betting odds to win the 2016 election, followed by Jeb Bush at 9/1).

The second key to making great people decisions is to carefully assess candidates against the most relevant competencies for the job. But we all know that's not what happens in elections today. People vote for candidates based not on essential criteria but on the superficial issues highlighted in stump speeches, television ads, and highly emotional, artificial public debates. In 2000, when George W. Bush was elected, didn't the United States need a president with global exposure and intercultural sensitivity? So why didn't voters consider his limited score on those dimensions? And what was the cost of that oversight?

Part of the problem is our tendency to choose people who are similar and familiar and make us feel comfortable. But we're actually worse at making political decisions than we are at everyday people choices because we're even more likely to tune relevant information out. Researchers at UCLA have used fMRI (functional magnetic resonance imaging) to measure people's neural activity as they listen to political statements on hot-button issues and are asked to agree or disagree.[1] The images show that the *most* politically sophisticated individuals actually use the *fewest* cognitive areas to "vote," showing the highest levels of activity in the *default state network* (specifically, the precuneus and dorsomedial prefrontal cortex) of the brain, which typically dominates when we're doing nothing, with no specific goals or tasks at hand. In other words, exposure to politics actually makes us worse at choosing our politicians!

That's pretty distressing news, because these decisions have huge impact. In his book *Indispensable: When Leaders Really Matter*, Harvard Business School professor Gautam Mukunda uses a variety of case studies from Abraham Lincoln to Winston Churchill to show how a single individual at the right place in the right time can save or destroy a country, and even change the course of world history.[2] Mukunda categorized these leaders into two groups: *filtered leaders* were typically insiders whose career followed a normal progression, while *unfiltered leaders* were either outsiders who had little experience or got their jobs through exceptional circumstances. While highly filtered leaders achieved little change, unfiltered ones had the most impact—for good (Mukunda cites Lincoln and Churchill), bad (Warren Harding), and evil (Adolf Hitler).

The obvious solution is to properly filter the unfiltered: consider many candidates, including insiders and outsiders, and carefully assess them against the required competencies. Any country leader should have, for example, a selfless motivation to improve the lives of others and the ability to put together and properly lead great teams. The characteristics and skills needed will, however, depend on the times: Churchill wasn't a distinguished politician between World Wars I and II, but the British counted themselves incredibly lucky to have him in charge when the latter broke out. If those responsible for giving leaders their power check for the right fit, neither the Hardings nor the Hitlers will make it through at *any time*, but the Lincolns and Churchills will *at the right time*.

To succeed by surrounding yourself with the best, you start with your immediate team and then, as a leader, try to help your organization improve its practices. But your country's people decisions also matter, for you and those around you. If you have the privilege to vote, resist your instinct to stick with the familiar and stay on autopilot. Think hard about society's challenges and the key competencies your top leader needs now. And, if you are in an influential position, go out of your way to promote the same open and critical attitude within your party and the general population. Democracy is an opportunity. Use it wisely.

# Singapore and Jamaica

Back in 1965, Jamaica and Singapore were identical twins: both subtropical islands of similar size and population, both recently emancipated British colonies, both very weak economies with comparably low income per capita.

Fifty years later, Singapore has become one of the most competitive nations on earth, with an income per capita higher than $60,000, the fourth-highest in the world. Meanwhile, Jamaica remains a third-world state, with an income per capita of less than $7,000, which puts it in 101st place.[1]

Each time I visit Singapore, I marvel at its extraordinary evolution, and I smile—because I know that its success stems not from *how* it is led (indeed, it started as a benign dictatorship and only slowly evolved through the decades to a much more open and democratic government) or *what* it has (no natural resources to speak of) but from *who* the country has attracted, developed, and put to work on its behalf. Singapore thrives because it passionately and consistently invests in talent, both in the private and public sector.

As in the cases of Amazon and Vale, the spark was an extraordinary leader with a clear vision. Immediately after the transition to independence, Prime Minister Lee Kuan Yew gave a speech to senior civil servants that clarified his grand ambitions: "Singapore must get some of [the] best in each year's crop of graduates into government," he said.[2] He explained that he wanted them to look at not just academic results but also imagination, quality of leadership, dynamism and, especially, character and motivation. Over the next several years, the country's public sector instituted massive scholarship programs; rigorous assessment practices focused on potential; extensive development and training, including exemplary rotations and milestone courses; and outstanding promotion, recognition, and salary benchmarking practices to match private employers.[3] The result, according to Harvard Business School's Michael Porter, is a highly efficient civil service elite that can dynamically shift policies and priorities over time, performing well against anything the world throws at them.[4]

High-quality, forward-thinking public leadership has in turn made Singapore more attractive to private-sector companies and talent. A few years ago, I was extremely pleased to meet with a government task force and discuss all the steps the country was taking to become not just a *host* but a *home* to the best foreign organizations and workers. And all those policies seem to be bearing fruit. One large textile industry supplier I know recently decided to move its headquarters from Switzerland to Singapore. And, according to the British CEO who told me about the switch, the members of the company's management committee have *all* agreed to relocate with their families—a testament to how hospitable an environment Singapore is perceived to be.

Another telling story comes from the German-born chief HR officer of a major global chemical company, who used to live in the country. One day he approached a cleaner at Changi Airport to ask if he could throw some unwanted papers in his cart. The man said yes, thanked the executive for properly disposing of his trash, and then said: "We welcome foreign talent in Singapore." When a humble cleaner understands the crucial importance of attracting and retaining the best people to his country, you know political leaders are doing something right.

By finding and investing in top talent, Singapore's political and public leaders have created a social and economic miracle, overcoming both the country's difficult history and its lack of natural resources and economies of scale. All other nations, including those that are much more favored, should strive to do the same.[5]

# The Pope

When I heard the news, I couldn't believe it: on February 11, 2013, Pope Benedict XVI announced his resignation, the first Pope to do so in six hundred years. As a devout Catholic and lifetime student and practitioner of great people decisions, I instantly had a crazy thought: Perhaps this was a once-in-a-lifetime opportunity for me. Maybe I could influence the appointment of his successor!

My first idea was to travel to the Vatican in person to meet with the 118 electing cardinals before the selection process, but I quickly learned that, challenging logistics aside, that sort of interaction is forbidden under conclave rules. Plan B was to try to reach them through the media and my professional network instead. I promptly wrote a blog called "How to Pick the Next Pope" for HBR.org and sent a similar message highlighting the importance of great leadership in the Catholic Church—for people of all faiths—to all eighteen hundred of my Egon Zehnder colleagues around the world.[1] I asked everyone, as long as they felt comfortable, to kindly forward the link or e-mail to anyone they thought might have a connection to one of the cardinals. Finally, I met the very impressive Apostolic

Nuncio in Buenos Aires; gave him a long letter, including a page of bullet points with my essential recommendations; and asked him to send it up the line to the electors at the Vatican.

The main point I made in all three outreach attempts was that no one is fully prepared to be the Pope. The job is vastly different from the ones done by the next highest-ranking church officials, just as the CEO role is nothing like that of a C-level executive. The Pope is alone at the top, with no peers, and no day-to-day boss (other than God, who happens to be a master delegator). He has to decide on all sorts of complex issues in an increasingly volatile global environment, facing enormous pressure. Meanwhile, the cardinals choosing the new Pope face significant constraints, including a fixed pool of candidates—themselves. It's an unusual process in which the recruiters are the potential hires and the direct reports choose their own future leader.

Of course, I knew there could be no change to the candidate pool or the election process in the month between Pope Benedict's announcement and the selection of his successor. But I wanted the cardinals to at least make sure to consider the right criteria for a great Pope, on top of the essential ones: deep faith, love for God, and a virtuous life. Up to that point, speculation on leading candidates had centered on the geographic region they represented. Three-quarters of Catholics live in the developing world: would the cardinals pick a Pope to reflect that? My advice was to instead focus on the factors that have been proven to predict leadership success.

First, the right *motivation*. Would the cardinals find a candidate with the purest blend of commitment and humility? Someone devoted to making our world a better place and building lasting greatness for truly selfless reasons?

Second, the *four key leadership assets* that indicate someone's *potential* to thrive in a much bigger, more complex role: curiosity, insight, engagement, and determination. Could the cardinals identify someone who seeks new experiences, ideas, knowledge, and self-awareness; who solicits feedback; and who stays open to learning and change? Someone able to gather and make sense of new information and to use his insights to shift legacy views and set new directions? Someone who connects on an emotional level with others, demonstrating empathy, communicating a persuasive vision, and inspiring commitment to the broader organization? Someone with the strength to persist in the face of difficulties and to bounce back from major setbacks or adversity?

Third, the *ability to make great people decisions*. This is particularly crucial in the Catholic Church, given its flat structure (forty-four hundred bishops reporting directly to the Pope), huge reach and geographic spread. Delegation is key. In addition, most bishops are appointed for life, so you can't remove them as easily as managers in a corporation. Any potential new Pope therefore had to have a solid track record of "who" choices. Had he promoted stars and worked to reassign or develop underperformers? Fostered diversity and inclusion? Consistently mentored great successors throughout his career?

In my long letter to the electing cardinals, I respectfully reminded them how Catholic leaders had pioneered exceptional people practices five centuries ago, highlighting Saint Ignatius from Loyola, the first leader of the Jesuits, who went out of his way to recruit, educate, train, and coach the very best talent and created a hugely influential institution in the process.

When the new Pope—an Argentine from Buenos Aires, the first pontiff from the Americas and the first from the southern hemisphere—was appointed, some colleagues believed I was a kingmaker. It was, of course, sheer coincidence; I hadn't assessed or recommended Jorge Mario Bergoglio or any other specific candidates.

Only time will reveal the legacy of Pope Francis. But I feel good about confirming that in his first year, as I write this, he seems to live up to the standards I set out above. He looks off the chart in terms of *motivation* (with an amazing level of humility, particularly given the reputation Buenos Aires citizens like me have for our big egos!). My favorite story so far is not his rejection of the red shoes or his willingness to wash the feet of women and juvenile detainees but the fact that, shortly after being elected, he personally called his newspaper deliveryman to cancel his subscription and thank him for his years of service. People who know the new Pope well tell me he also scores very high in each of the four indicators of executive *potential* (curiosity, insight, engagement, and determination) and that, as a Jesuit (the first to be elected Pope), he doesn't hesitate to make brave leadership changes.

Whether my messages made it to them or not, so far the cardinals appear to have made a good choice. And it's one we all can learn from. Unfortunately, in our social organizations, we very rarely make people decisions with the same discipline and rigor that we apply in the corporate world. We become much more passive and tolerant of mediocrity. But many of the most influential groups in the world are not businesses, and those that do follow best practices for talent can have huge impact for centuries. Think about the Jesuits' extraordinary influence on education over the past five hundred years, building what would by the late eighteenth century become the world's largest higher-education network, with seven hundred institutions sprawled across five continents. Contrast that with the typical *Fortune* 500 company, which has a less than 20 percent chance of surviving one century.[2]

So the next time you get involved in a social initiative—be it your child's school; your church, synagogue, or mosque; a community club; foundation; or NGO—consider what could be proactively done to help the organization attract the best and strengthen its leadership. If we only have successful companies, we will have a prosperous society, but not a great one.[3] Encourage all the groups you influence to start making better "who" decisions too.

# Conclusion

The first era of people decisions lasted millennia. For thousands of years, humans made their choices about each other based on physical strength. If you wanted to erect a pyramid, dig a canal, fight a war, harvest a crop—even partner with someone to raise a family—you chose the fittest, the healthiest, the strongest you could find. These attributes were easy to assess, and, despite their growing irrelevance in today's world, we still unconsciously look for them: *Fortune* 500 CEOs are on average 2.5 inches taller than the average American, and the statistics on military leaders and country presidents are similar.[1]

I was born and raised during the second era of people decisions, which emphasized intelligence, experience, and performance. By the early twentieth century, IQ—verbal, analytical, mathematical, and logical cleverness—had justifiably become an important factor in the selection process (particularly for white-collar roles), with educational pedigrees (if not tests) used as a proxy for measuring it. Much labor also became standardized and professionalized. Workers such as engineers and accountants could be certified with reliability and transparency, and since most jobs (from company to company, industry to industry, year to year) were relatively similar, we all thought past performance was the best predictor of future performance. If you were looking for an engineer or accountant, a lawyer or designer, even a CEO, you would scout out and interview the best, most experienced engineers, accountants, lawyers, designers, or CEOs.

I joined the executive search profession in the 1980s at the start of the third era of people decisions, which was driven by the competency movement still prevalent today. David McClelland's 1973 paper "Testing for Competence Rather Than for 'Intelligence'" proposed that workers, and especially managers, be evaluated on specific characteristics or skills proven to differentiate typical from outstanding performance in the roles for which they were being hired.[2] The time was right for such thinking because technological evolution and industry convergence had made jobs much more complex and unique, often rendering experience and performance in previous positions irrelevant. So instead, we started decomposing work into competencies and looking for candidates with the right combination of intelligence, skills, and other attributes to match. For leadership roles, research also began to show the importance of emotional intelligence over IQ.

I believe we're now witnessing the dawn of a fourth era of people decisions, in which the focus is rapidly shifting to potential, or our ability to grow and adapt to fundamentally different and increasingly complex responsibilities. Geopolitics, business, industries, and jobs are changing so rapidly that we can't predict the competencies needed to succeed even a few years out. It is therefore imperative to identify and develop those with a strong motivation to be the best they can be and contribute to something larger than themselves; an insatiable curiosity that propels them to explore new avenues and ideas; keen insight that allows them to see connections where others don't; a high level engagement with their work and the people around them; and the determination to overcome setbacks and obstacles. (That doesn't mean forgetting about factors like intelligence, experience, performance, and specific competencies, particularly the ones related to leadership; but potential should now be higher on your priority list.)

Potential is, of course, much harder to gauge than all those other attributes. And it can be harder to find, not least because of the "other GDP" factors causing talent pools to shrink. But when you are deliberate about looking for it, determined to overcome all the obstacles your brain, education, organization, and society put in your way, energetic about developing and leading the talent you've identified, smart about putting the right mix of teammates together, and willing to bring this rigor to every people decision you make in every realm of your life, you will put yourself at a huge advantage. Not only will you be able to identify and surround yourself with the best, you'll also be able to bring out the best in them, in yourself, in your organization, and in your world.

So let me end this book with a call to action. Your quest going forward is to consider everyone around you with fresh eyes, to tirelessly search for and diligently nurture potential, and to enthusiastically direct those with whom you've surrounded yourself toward collective greatness. This is the surest path toward personal and professional fulfillment and prosperity.

# Notes

## Introduction

1. Some basic information on Jeff Bezos can be found in "Jeff Bezos," *Wikipedia*, http://en.wikipedia.org/wiki/Jeff_Bezos; and, "Jeff Bezos," *bio/ True Story*, http://www.biography.com/people/jeff-bezos-9542209. I also highly recommend reading the interview in "Interview: Jeff Bezos," *Academy of Achievement*, May 4, 2001, http://www.achievement.org/autodoc/printmember/bez0int-1.

2. "Jeff Bezos: The King of E-Commerce," *Entrepreneur*, October 9, 2008, http://www.entrepreneur.com/article/197608.

3. Amazon.com Inc., *Annual Report 2012* (pdf), http://www.annualreports.com/Company/1755.

4. Morten T. Hansen, Herminia Ibarra, and Urs Peyer, "100: The Best-Performing CEOs in the World," *Harvard Business Review*, January–February 2013, http://hbr.org/2013/01/the-best-performing-ceos-in-the-world.

5. Most of the information in this section comes from an interview of Roger Agnelli by the author, São Paulo, Brazil, April 2, 2013, followed by additional personal exchanges.

6. Vale, *Annual Reports 2001* and *2011*, http://www.vale.com/EN/investors/Annual-reports/20F/Pages/default.aspx.

7. Roger Agnelli's farewell speech, May 20, 2011.

8. Hansen, Ibarra, and Peyer, "100: The Best-Performing CEOs in the World."

9. Agnelli described his strategy and decision-making culture in an interview with my colleague, "Edilson Camara in Fit for the Future: How a New Decision-Making Culture Helped Brazilian Raw Materials Company CVRD Join the World's Leading Players," *THE FOCUS* 10, no. 1, 2006.

10. Jeff Bezos, interviewed by Julia Kirby and Thomas A. Stewart, "The Institutional Yes," *Harvard Business Review*, October 2007, http://hbr.org/2007/10/the-institutional-yes/ar/1.

11. In a 1998 Amazon Shareholder letter, Bezos reported that, "It would be impossible to produce results in an environment as dynamic as the Internet

without extraordinary people. Working to create a little bit of history isn't supposed to be easy, and, well, we're finding that things are as they're supposed to be! We now have a team of 2,100 smart, hard-working, passionate folks who put customers first. Setting the bar high in our approach to hiring has been, and will continue to be, the single most important element of Amazon.com's success." See http://www.cx-journey.com/2013/05/jeff-bezos-gets-customer-experience-but.html.

12. "Lesson #4: Create a High Hiring Bar," http://www.evancarmichael.com/Famous-Entrepreneurs/959/Lesson-4-Create-a-High-Hiring-Bar.html.

13. As reported in 2012 by CNN Money on November 16, 2012, http://management.fortune.cnn.com/2012/11/16/jeff-bezos-amazon/. Bezos has an extraordinarily loyal, long-serving, and close-knit brain trust of top executives who can channel his authority inside and outside the company. Wilke, the North American consumer chief, is a 13-year veteran. Jeff Blackburn, a former investment banker who worked on Amazon's IPO before joining the company in 1998, is Bezos' top dealmaker. And Web services chief Andy Jassy is a Bezos protégé who joined the company in 1997.

14. As reported by Bloomberg on April 1, 2011, and Exame on March 31, 2011, the Brazilian government, which owned 61 percent of the company's controlling share, precipitated Agnelli's departure (see http://www.bloomberg.com/news/print/2011-04-01/vale-s-main-shareholders-group-seeking-replacement-for-ceo-roger-agnelli.html and http://exame.abril.com.br/revista-exame/edicoes/0989/noticias/4-milhoes-de-investidores-pagam-a-conta). Within a year, seven out of the eight members of the company's executive committee had also left. Within two years, the company had lost almost half of its value (see http://www.bloomberg.com/news/2012-12-10/agnelli-bets-on-metals-after-leading-vale-boom-corporate-brazil.html). There were several reasons for the decline, including investors' growing disenchanted with Brazilian stocks and a decline in commodity prices, yet Vale's market value loss during that period was much larger than those of its closest competitors, such as Rio Tinto and BHP. But it's clear that the loss of an outstanding leadership team and worries about political interference with future appointments and business decisions also played a role.

15. Walter Isaacson, "The Real Leadership Lessons of Steve Jobs," *Harvard Business Review*, April 2012, http://hbr.org/2012/04/the-real-leadership-lessons-of-steve-jobs/.

16. "Steve Jobs Interview: One-on-One in 1995," *Computerworld*, October 6, 2011, http://www.computerworld.com/s/article/9220609/Steve_Jobs_interview_One_on_one_in_1995.

17. Ibid.

18. Ibid.

19. "Jonathan Ive," *Wikipedia*, http://en.wikipedia.org/wiki/Jonathan_Ive.

20. Isaacson, "The Real Leadership Lessons of Steve Jobs."

21. "Steve Jobs Interview."

22. Although it's not easy to find a lot of public information about Samsung and other major Korean companies, I was able to get unique insights about them when launching the Korean version of my first book, *Great People Decisions: Why They Matter So Much, Why They Are So Hard, and How You Can Master Them* (Hoboken, NJ: John Wiley & Sons, 2007) and from my Egon Zehnder colleagues in Korea, including Simon Kim, Eugene Kim, Julius Kim and Yoonmi Eom.

## Chapter 1

1. Nigel Nicholson, *Managing the Human Animal* (Cheshire, UK: Texere Publishing, 2000).

2. Mark van Vugt and Anjana Ahuja, *Naturally Selected: The Evolutionary Science of Leadership* (New York: HarperCollins Publishers, 2010).

3. Shankar Vedantam, *The Hidden Brain: How Our Unconscious Minds Elect Presidents, Control Markets, Wage Wars, and Save Our Lives* (New York: Spiegel & Grau, 2010), 62.

4. Neha Mahajan, Zoe Liberman, and Karen Wynn, press release, Association for Psychological Science, March 12, 2013, http://www.psychologicalscience.org/index.php/news/releases/babies-prefer-individuals-who-harm-those-that-arent-like-them.html.

5. Ken Robinson, www.ted.com/talks/ken_robinson_says_schools_kill_creativity.html (February 2006).

6. Rakesh Khurana, *From Higher Aims to Hired Hands, the Social Transformation of American Business Schools and the Unfulfilled Promise of Management as a Profession* (Princeton: Princeton University Press, 2007), 169.

7. Robert S. Rubin and Erich C. Dierdorff, *Academy of Management Learning & Education*, 8, no. 2 (2009): 208–224.

8. Daniel Goleman, *Leadership: The Power of Emotional Intelligence* (Northampton, MA: More Than Sound LLC, 2011), 99.

## Chapter 2

1. Daniel Kahneman, *Thinking, Fast and Slow,* 1st ed. (New York: Farrar, Straus and Giroux, 2013), 261–262.

2. Ibid., 85–88.

## Chapter 3

1. In one of the most comprehensive global surveys of corporate director attitudes about their companies' talent management practices, Harvard Business School's Boris Groysberg and Deborah Bell found that scores for

"getting the wrong people off the bus," were by far the lowest across the nine dimensions studied. This was consistent across all geographies: even in North America, Australia, and New Zealand, where practices were rated higher than in the rest of the world, fewer than 10 percent of board members rated their companies as effective in this category. See http://blogs.hbr.org/2013/05/talent-management-boards-give/.

2. See http://www.youtube.com/watch?v=xD_CMKLL8GU and http://m.npr.org/news/Arts+%26+Life/136495499.

3. Daniel Kahneman, *Thinking, Fast and Slow,* 1st ed. (New York: Farrar, Straus and Giroux, 2013), 283–286.

4. William N. Thorndike Jr., *The Outsiders: Eight Unconventional CEOs and Their Radically Rational Blueprint for Success* (Boston: Harvard Business Review Press, 2012), 114.

## Chapter 4

1. Rakesh Khurana and Nitin Nohria, "The Performance Impact of New CEOs," *MIT Sloan Management Review* (Winter 2001); cited in Claudio Fernández-Aráoz, *Great People Decisions* (Hoboken, NJ: John Wiley & Sons, Inc., 2007), 163.

2. Fernández-Aráoz, *Great People Decisions,* 165, and http://citeseerx.ist.psu.edu/viewdoc/download?doi=10.1.1.201.2749&rep=rep1&type=pdf.

3. Fernández-Aráoz, *Great People Decisions,* 163–166.

4. James S. Ang and Gregory Leo Nagel, *The Effect of CEO Hiring Source on Total Cash Flow,* May 19, 2012, http://ssrn.com/abstract=2018996.

5. Fernández-Aráoz, *Great People Decisions,* 166.

## Chapter 5

1. Malcolm Gladwell, *Blink: The Power of Thinking without Thinking* (Boston: Little, Brown, 2005), 73–74.

2. Suzy Welch, *10-10-10: A Fast and Powerful Way to Get Unstuck in Love, at Work, and with Your Family* (New York: Scribner, 2009).

## Chapter 6

1. Ben Bryant, "Judges Are More Lenient after Taking a Break, Study Finds," *The Guardian,* April 11, 2011.

2. Reported in John Tierney, "Do You Suffer from Decision Fatigue?" *New York Times,* August 17, 2011.

3. Ibid.

# Chapter 7

1. Claudio Fernández-Aráoz, Boris Groysberg, and Nitin Nohria, "The Definitive Guide to Recruiting in Good Times and Bad," *Harvard Business Review,* May 2009.

2. As reported by Howard Martin, Global Consumer Products Sector Leader of Ernst & Young, estimates show that 70 percent of world growth over the next few years will come from emerging markets, with China and India accounting for 40 percent of that growth ("Emerging Markets Increase Their Global Power," http://www.ey.com/GL/en/Issues/Business-environment/Six-global-trends-shaping-the-business-world---Emerging-markets-increase-their-global-power).

The International Monetary Fund (IMF) forecasts that the total GDP of emerging markets could overtake that of the developed economies as early as 2014. The forecasts suggest that investors will continue to invest in emerging markets for some time to come. The emerging markets already attract almost 50 percent of foreign direct investment (FDI) global inflows and account for 25 percent of FDI outflows. The brightest spots for FDI continue to be Africa; the Middle East; and Brazil, Russia, India, and China (the BRICs). By 2020, the BRICs are expected to account for nearly 50 percent of all global GDP growth. In 2009 already emerging-to-emerging (E2E) trade had reached US$2.9 trillion. This massive flow of investment among emerging markets is well on its way to creating a second tier of emerging market leaders.

Other data from "KPMG Survey: U.S. Companies to Increase Investment Across a Broader Range of Emerging Markets to Drive Growth," http://www.kpmg.com/us/en/issuesandinsights/articlespublications/press-releases/pages/kpmg-survey-us-companies-to-increase-investment-across-a-broader-range-of-emerging-markets-to-drive-growth.aspx; and *Fortresses and Footholds Emerging Market Growth Strategies, Practices and Outlook,* http://www.deloitte.com/assets/Dcom-UnitedStates/Local%20Assets/Documents/us_consulting_Fortresses%20and%20Footholds_111511.pdf.

3. "Emerging Markets Increase Their Global Power."

4. "Demographic Shifts Transform the Global Workforce," http://www.ey.com/GL/en/Issues/Business-environment/Six-global-trends-shaping-the-business-world---Demographic-shifts-transform-the-global-workforce.

5. Boris Groysberg, "Assessing the Leadership Bench," http://www.exed.hbs.edu/assets/Documents/qa-dptm-groysberg.pdf.

6. Boris Groysberg and Deborah Bell, "Talent Management: Boards Give Their Companies an 'F,'" *HBR Blog Network,* May 28, 2013, blogs.hbr.org/2013/05/talent-management-boards-give/.

7. Boris Groysberg and Deborah Bell, "New Research: Where the Talent Wars Are Hottest," *HBR Blog Network,* June 21, 2013, http://blogs.hbr.org/2013/06/new-research-where-the-talent/.

## Chapter 8

1. Claudio Fernández-Aráoz, *Great People Decisions* (Hoboken, NJ: John Wiley & Sons, Inc., 2007), 38–40.

2. Ernest O'Boyle Jr. and Herman Aguinis, "The Best and the Rest: Revisiting the Norm of Normality of Individual Performance," *Personnel Psychology* 65, no. 1 (2012): 79–119.

3. Michael Mankins, Alan Bird, and James Root, "Making Star Teams Out of Star Players," *Harvard Business Review,* January–February 2013.

4. Nassim Nicholas Taleb, *The Black Swan: The Impact of the Highly Improbable* (New York: Random House, 2007).

5. O'Boyle and Aguinis, "The Best and the Rest."

## Chapter 9

1. There are many advantages to depression in addition to more realistic assessments of your strengths and weaknesses. For an excellent discussion, see Jonah Lehrer, "Depression's Upside," *New York Times,* February 28, 2010.

2. Daniel Kahneman, *Thinking, Fast and Slow,* 1st ed. (New York: Farrar, Straus and Giroux, 2013), 255–265.

3. Cited in David Dunning, Chip Heath, and Jerry M. Suls, "Flawed Self-Assessment, Implications for Health, Education, and the Workplace," *Psychological Science in the Public Interest* 5, no. 3 (December 2004): 69–106.

4. Cited in Chip Heath and Dan Heath, *Decisive: How to Make Better Choices in Life and Work* (New York: Crown Business, 2013), 212–216.

## Chapter 10

1. Robert J. Thornton, *The Lexicon of Intentionally Ambiguous Recommendation: Positive-Sounding References for People Who Can't Manage Their Own Sock Drawer* (Naperville, IL: Sourcebooks, 2003).

2. Carmen Nobel, "How to Spot a Liar," *HBS Working Knowledge,* May 13, 2013.

3. M. Reinhard, M. Scharmach, and P. Müller, "It's Not What You Are, It's What You Know: Experience, Beliefs, and the Detection of Deception in Employment Interviews," *Journal of Applied Social Psychology* 43, no. 3 (2013): 467–479, http://dx.doi.org/10.1111/j.1559-1816.2013.01011.x.

## Chapter 11

1. *Monkeys Beat Market Cap Indices,* Cass Business School, April 4, 2013, http://www.cass.city.ac.uk/news-and-events/news/2013/april/monkeys-beat-market-cap-indices.

## Chapter 12

1. R. Taft, "The Ability to Judge People," *Psychological Bulletin* 52, no. 1 (1955): 1–23.

## Chapter 13

1. Peter Drucker, "How to Make People Decisions" *Harvard Business Review,* July–August 1985.

2. Jack Welch and Suzy Welch, "The Hiring Batting Average," *Bloomberg-BusinessWeek,* July 19, 2007, http://www.businessweek.com/stories/2007-08-19/the-hiring-batting-average.

3. Ibid.

4. Claudio Fernández-Aráoz, "Making People Decisions in the New Global Environment," *MIT Sloan Management Review* 49, no. 1 (Fall 2007): 17–20.

## Chapter 14

1. "Dayak People," *Wikipedia,* http://en.wikipedia.org/wiki/Dayak_people.

## Chapter 15

1. Claudio Fernández-Aráoz, *Great People Decisions* (Hoboken, NJ: John Wiley & Sons, Inc., 2007), 170–173.

2. Chip Heath and Dan Heath, *Decisive: How to Make Better Choices in Life and Work* (New York: Crown Business, 2013).

3. Cited in ibid., 37

4. Cited in ibid., 57.

5. Cited in ibid., 56.

## Chapter 16

1. Daniel Kahneman, *Thinking, Fast and Slow,* 1st ed. (New York: Farrar, Straus and Giroux, 2013), 226–227.

2. Atul Gawande, *The Checklist Manifesto: How to Get Things Right* (New York: Metropolitan Books, 2009).

3. Kahneman, *Thinking, Fast and Slow*, 229–232.

4. Ibid., 222–223.

5. Ibid., 230–232.

6. Claudio Fernández-Aráoz, *Great People Decisions* (Hoboken, NJ: John Wiley & Sons, Inc., 2007), 94–97 and 105–108.

7. Robyn M. Dawes, "The Robust Beauty of Improper Linear Models in Decision Making," *American Psychologist* 34, no. 7 (1979): 571–582.

8. Kahneman, *Thinking, Fast and Slow*, 231.

## Chapter 17

1. "Ted Williams," National Baseball Hall of Fame and Museum, http://baseballhall.org/hof/williams-ted.

2. "Ted Williams," *Wikipedia*, http://en.wikipedia.org/wiki/Ted_Williams.

3. Tom Verducci, "What Happened to Ted?" *Sports Illustrated*, August 12, 2003, http://sportsillustrated.cnn.com/baseball/news/2003/08/12/williams_si/.

4. Randolfe H. Wicker, "Cloning Ted Williams," http://www.clonerights.com/new_page_9.htm.

5. Martin E.P. Seligman, Ph.D., *What You Can Change . . . and What You Can't: The Complete Guide to Successful Self-Improvement* (New York: Ballantine Publishing Group, 1993).

6. Jim Collins, "Filling the Seats: How People Decisions Help Build a Great Company," keynote topic in *THE FOCUS* 10, no. 1, May, 2006.

## Chapter 18

1. Nando Parrado, "Homepage," www.parrado.com. A wonderful account of the drama in the Andes is told by another survivor, Nando Parrado, in his book *Miracle in the Andes: 72 Days on the Mountain and My Long Trek Home* (New York: Crown Publishers, 2006).

2. Pedro Algorta, "Homepage," www.pedroalgorta.es/en/.

## Chapter 19

1. The original experiment is described in http://en.wikipedia.org/wiki/Stanford_marshmallow_experiment. Other more recent related and follow-up studies, including: "The Marshmallow Study Revisited: Delaying Gratification Depends as Much On Nurture as On Nature," *Science Daily*, October 11, 2012, http://www.sciencedaily.com/releases/2012/10/121011090655.htm; Sarah Kliff, "The Marshmallow

Test, Revisited," *Washington Post,* updated October 13, 2012, http://
www.washingtonpost.com/blogs/wonkblog/wp/2012/10/13/the-
marshmallow-test-revisited/; Celeste Kidd, Holly Palmeri, Richard N.
Aslin, "Rational Snacking: Young Children's Decision-Making on the
Marshmallow Task Is Moderated by Beliefs about Environmental
Reliability," 2012, http://www.bcs.rochester.edu/people/ckidd/papers/
KiddPalmeriAslin2012_Cognition.pdf; Drake Bennett, "What Does the
Marshmallow Test Actually Test?," *Bloomberg Businessweek,* October 17,
2012, http://www.businessweek.com/articles/2012-10-17/what-does-
the-marshmallow-test-actually-test; "Quitting Marshmallow Test Can Be a
Rational Decision," *Science Daily,* March 26, 2013, http://www.sciencedaily
.com/releases/2013/03/130326194138.htm; "Marshmallow Test Points to
Biological Basis for Delayed Gratification," *Science Daily,* September 1, 2011,
http://www.sciencedaily.com/releases/2011/08/110831160220.htm; "New
Paper Pinpoints a Seat of Self-Control in the Brain," *Science Daily,* March 31,
2010, http://www.sciencedaily.com/releases/2010/03/100330161843.
htm; "Why Delaying Gratification Is Smart," *Science Daily,* September 11,
2008, http://www.sciencedaily.com/releases/2008/09/080909111022.
htm; "Children's Self-Control Is Associated with Their Body Mass Index
as Adults," *Science Daily,* August 16, 2012, http://www.sciencedaily.com/
releases/2012/08/120816075413.htm.

2. Daniel Goleman, *Emotional Intelligence* (New York: Bantam Books,
1995).

# Chapter 20

1. For a great introduction to the topic of portability, see Boris Groysberg, Ashish Nanda, and Nitin Nohria, "The Risky Business of Hiring Stars,"
*Harvard Business Review,* May 2004, http://hbr.org/2004/05/the-risky-
business-of-hiring-stars/ar/1 and Boris Groysberg, Andrew N. McLean, and
Nitin Nohria, "Are Leaders Portable?" *Harvard Business Review,* May 2006,
http://hbr.org/2006/05/are-leaders-portable/ar/1. For a more thorough
discussion, I also highly recommend Boris Groysberg, *Chasing Stars: The Myth
of Talent and the Portability of Performance* (Princeton: Princeton University
Press, 2010).

2. GE has been for many years the company that produces the largest
number of CEOs, while McKinsey is the company that gives you the highest
odds of becoming a CEO (while it has produced less CEOs than GE, it has a
much lower number of employees), *USA Today,* September 1, 2008, http://
usatoday30.usatoday.com/money/companies/management/2008-01-08-ceo-
companies_n.htm).

3. Groysberg, McLean, and Nohria, "Are Leaders Portable?"

# Chapter 21

1. Claudio Fernández-Aráoz, "Why I Like People with Unconventional Résumés," *HBR* Blog *Network,* July 2, 2012, http://blogs.hbr.org/2012/07/why-i-like-people-with-unconve/.

# Chapter 22

1. Michael J. Mauboussin, *The Success Equation: Untangling Skill and Luck in Business, Sports and Investing* (Boston: Harvard Business Review Press, 2012).

2. Noam T. Wasserman, N. Nohria, and Bharat N. Anand, "When Does Leadership Matter? The Contingent Opportunities View of CEO Leadership," working paper no. 01-063 (Boston: Harvard Business School, April 2001).

3. Asmus Komm et al., *Return on Leadership—Competencies That Generate Growth,* Egon Zehnder International and McKinsey & Co., February 2011, http://www.egonzehnder.com/us/leadership-insights/leadership-strategy-services/competencies-that-generate-growth-return-on-leadership.html; and Katharina Herrmann, Asmus Komm, and Sven Smit, "Do You Have the Right Leaders for Your Growth Strategies?" *McKinsey Quarterly,* July 2011, http://www.mckinsey.com/insights/leading_in_the_21st_century/do_you_have_the_right_leaders_for_your_growth_strategies.

# Chapter 23

1. The following link introduces Hofstede's cultural dimensions theory: http://en.wikipedia.org/wiki/Hofstede's_cultural_dimensions_theory. Another useful framework to analyze cultural differences at work is presented by Fons Trompenaars and Charles Hampden-Turner, *Riding the Waves of Culture: Understanding Diversity in Global Business* (New York: McGraw-Hill, 2012). Finally, a useful resource for the design and implementation of global selection systems is Anne Marie Ryan and Nancy Tippins, *Designing and Implementing Global Selection Systems* (Malden, MA: Wiley-Blackwell, 2009).

# Chapter 24

1. "Transplant Rejection," *Wikipedia,* http://en.wikipedia.org/wiki/Transplant_rejection.

2. Boris Groysberg, *Chasing Stars* (Princeton, NJ: Princeton University Press, 2010).

3. Michael Watkins, *The First 90 Days: Proven Strategies for Getting Up to Speed Faster and Smarter,* updated and expanded ed. (Boston: Harvard Business School Publishing, 2013).

4. Also see Claudio Fernández-Aráoz, *Great People Decisions* (Hoboken, NJ: John Wiley & Sons, Inc., 2007), chapter 9; and John J. Gabarro, *The Dynamics of Taking Charge* (Boston: Harvard Business School Press, 1987).

5. Cassie Rodenberg, "Next-Gen Transplant Techniques Can Stop Organ Rejection," *Popular Mechanics,* January 28, 2010, http://www.popularmechanics .com/science/health/life-extension/4343954.

## Chapter 25

1. See http://www.amazon.com/Sophies-Choice-William-Styron/ dp/0679736379 and http://www.imdb.com/title/tt0084707/.

2. John W. Gardner, *Excellence* (1961; rev. New York: W.W. Norton & Company, Inc., 1984).

3. Jean Martin and Conrad Schmidt, "How to Keep Your Top Talent," *Harvard Business Review,* May 2010, 54–61, http://www.harvardbusiness.org/ how-keep-your-top-talent.

4. Claudio Fernández-Aráoz, Boris Groysberg, and Nitin Nohria, "How to Hang On to Your High Potentials," *Harvard Business Review,* October 2011, http://hbr.org/2011/10/how-to-hang-on-to-your-high-potentials.

5. *Executive Education in Corporate America: A Report on Practices and Trends in 300 Leading Companies in Eight Major Industries* (Palatine, IL: Executive Knowledgeworks, Anthony J. Fresina & Associates, Inc., 1988).

6. "Notable & Quotable," *Wall Street Journal,* April 4, 2013, http://online .wsj.com/article/SB10001424127887324100904578403011865246292.html.

## Chapter 26

1. Daniel Goleman, *Leadership: The Power of Emotional Intelligence* (Northampton, MA: More Than Sound LLC, 2011), 99.

2. Richard Boyatzis, Elizabeth C. Stubbs, and Scott N. Taylor, "Learning Cognitive and Emotional Intelligence Competencies through Graduate Management Education," *Academy of Management Learning and Education* 1, no. 2 (2002): 150–162.

3. Daniel Goleman, Richard Boyatzis, and Annie McKee, *Primal Leadership: Realizing the Power of Emotional Intelligence* (Boston: Harvard Business School Press, 2002), 91–112. Other excellent papers that discuss the latest findings on developing emotional and social competencies, including the emotional neuroendocrine aspects of learning, are: Ronald J. Burke, Cary L. Cooper, *Inspiring Leaders* (New York: Routledge, 2006), 119–131; Richard E. Boyatzis et al., "Examination of the Neural Substrates Activated in Memories of Experiences with Resonant and Dissonant Leaders," *Leadership Quarterly* 23 (2012): 259–272; Anthony I. Jack et al., *NeuroImag* (2012, accepted manuscript);

Richard E. Boyatzis, "Leadership Development from a Complexity Perspective," *Consulting Psychology Journal: Practice and Research* 60, no. 4 (2008): 298–313; and Richard E. Boyatzis et al., "Coaching with Compassion: An fMRI Study of Coaching to the Positive or Negative Emotional Attractor," presented at the Academy of Management Annual Conference, Montreal, August 2010.

## Chapter 27

1. Morten T. Hansen, Herminia Ibarra, and Urs Peyer, "100: The Best-Performing CEOs in the World," *Harvard Business Review,* January–February 2013, http://hbr.org/2013/01/the-best-performing-ceos-in-the-world.

2. Ram Charan, Stephen Drotter, and James Noel, *The Leadership Pipeline: How to Build the Leadership Powered Company* (Hoboken, NJ: John Wiley & Sons, Inc., 2011).

## Chapter 28

1. Asmus Komm et al., *Return on Leadership—Competencies That Generate Growth,* Egon Zehnder International and McKinsey & Co., February 2011, http://www.egonzehnder.com/us/leadership-insights/leadership-strategy-services/competencies-that-generate-growth-return-on-leadership.html; and Katharina Herrmann, Asmus Komm, and Sven Smit, "Do You Have the Right Leaders for Your Growth Strategies?" *McKinsey Quarterly,* July 2011, http://www.mckinsey.com/insights/leading_in_the_21st_century/do_you_have_the_right_leaders_for_your_growth_strategies.

## Chapter 29

1. Frans de Waal, "Two Monkeys Were Paid Unequally," excerpt from TED Talk, April 4, 2013, http://www.youtube.com/watch?v=meiU6TxysCg.

2. Brian Knutson et al., "Nucleus Accumbens Activation Mediates the Influence of Reward Cues on Financial Risk-Taking," *Neuroreport* 19, no. 5 (March 2008): 509–513, http://mpra.ub.uni-muenchen.de/8013/.

3. Jim Collins, *Good to Great,* 1st ed. (New York: HarperCollins Publishers, Inc., 2001), 49 and 244–246.

4. Daniel H. Pink, *Drive: The Surprising Truth about What Motivates Us* (New York: Riverhead Books, 2009).

## Chapter 30

1. See Boris Groysberg, Andrew N. McLean, and Nitin Nohria, "Are Leaders Portable," *Harvard Business Review,* May 2006, http://hbr.org/2006/05/are-leaders-portable/ar/. This excellent article dramatically shows how about

half of formerly successful GE executives underperformed their respective sectors when hired as CEOs for a job where they had a poor fit.

## Chapter 31

1. Michael Mankins, Alan Bird, and James Root, "Making Star Teams Out of Star Players," *Harvard Business Review,* January–February 2013, http://hbr.org/2013/01/making-star-teams-out-of-star-players/ar/.

## Chapter 32

1. Nate Silver, *The Signal and the Noise: Why So Many Predictions Fail—but Some Don't* (New York: Penguin Press, 2012), 20–46.

## Chapter 33

1. Thomas Barta, Markus Kleiner, and Tilo Neuman, "Is There a Payoff from Top-Team Diversity?" *McKinsey Quarterly* (April 2012), http://www.mckinsey.com/insights/organization/is_there_a_payoff_from_top-team_diversity.

2. David A. Thomas and Robin J. Ely, "Making Differences Matter: A New Paradigm for Managing Diversity," *Harvard Business Review,* September 1996, http://hbr.org/1996/09/making-differences-matter-a-new-paradigm-for-managing-diversity/ar/1.

3. Marilyn Marks, "Blind Auditions Key to Hiring Musicians," *Princeton Weekly Bulletin,* February 12, 2001, http://www.princeton.edu/pr/pwb/01/0212/7b.shtml.

4. There are many wonderful contributions by Tamara Erickson, including *What's Next, Gen X?: Keeping Up, Moving Ahead, and Getting the Career You Want* (Boston: Harvard Business Press, 2010). I also recommend Jeanne C. Meister and Karie Willyerd, *The 2020 Workplace: How Innovative Companies Attract, Develop, and Keep Tomorrow's Employees Today* (New York: HarperCollins, 2010).

5. See http://en.wikipedia.org/wiki/Hofstede's_cultural_dimensions_theory.

## Chapter 34

1. "Hixonia Nyasulu," *Wikipedia,* http://en.wikipedia.org/wiki/Hixonia_Nyasulu.

2. Boris Groysberg, Kerry Herman, and Annelena Lobb, *Women MBAs at Harvard Business School: 1962–2012,* Harvard Business School Case 413-013 (Boston: Harvard Business School Publishing, March 2013).

3. Sylvia Ann Hewlett and Ripa Rashid, *Winning the War for Talent in Emerging Markets: Why Women Are the Solution* (Boston: Harvard Business Review Press, 2011).

4. Louann Brizendine, *The Female Brain* (New York: Broadway Books, 2006); Louann Brizendine, *The Male Brain* (New York: Broadway Books, 2010).

5. Sheryl Sandberg, *Lean In: Women, Work, and the Will to Lead* (New York: Alfred A. Knopf/ Borzoi Books, 2013).

6. Sandrine Devillard et al., *Women Matter: Making the Breakthrough*, McKinsey & Co., March 2012, http://www.mckinsey.com/client_service/organization/latest_thinking/women_matter.

7. Joanna Barsh, Susie Cranston, and Rebecca A. Craske, "Centered Leadership: How Talented Women Thrive," *McKinsey Quarterly* (September 2008), http://www.mckinsey.com/insights/leading_in_the_21st_century/centered_leadership_how_talented_women_thrive.

8. Tommaso Arenare, "Female Leadership, Italy, Diversity and the Beauty of Leading by Example," *Open Thinking* (blog), May 26, 2012, http://tommasoarenare.wordpress.com/2012/05/26/female-leadership-italy-diversity-and-the-beauty-of-leading-by-example/.

## Chapter 35

1. Eduardo P. Braun, "It's the Culture, Stupid!" *Huffington Post Blog*, June 25, 2013, http://www.huffingtonpost.com/eduardo-p-braun/its-the-culture-stupid_2_b_3487503.html.

2. Jon Katzenbach and DeAnne Aguirre, "Culture and the Chief Executive," *Strategy + Business*, May 28, 2013, http://www.strategy-business.com/article/00179?pg=all.

3. Ashish Nanda and Kelley Morrell, *Strategic Review at Egon Zehnder International (A)*, Harvard Business School case study (Boston: Harvard Business Publishing, August 2, 2004).

4. Richard E. Boyatzis et al., "Examination of the Neural Substrates Activated in Memories of Experiences with Resonant and Dissonant Leaders, *Leadership Quarterly* 23 (2012): 259–272; Richard E. Boyatzis et al., "Coaching with Compassion: An fMRI Study of Coaching to the Positive or Negative Emotional Attractor," presented at the Academy of Management Annual Conference, Montreal, August 2010.

## Chapter 36

1. Egon Zehnder, "A Simpler Way to Pay," *Harvard Business Review*, April 2001, http://hbr.org/2001/04/a-simpler-way-to-pay/ar/1.

2. Marshall W. Van Alstyne, "Create Colleagues, Not Competitors," *Harvard Business Review,* September 2005.

## Chapter 37

1. Christian Caspar, Ana Karina Dias, and Heinz-Peter Elstrodt, *The Five Attributes of Enduring Family Businesses,* McKinsey & Co., January 2010, http://www.mckinsey.com/insights/organization/the_five_attributes_of_enduring_family_businesses.

2. Morten Bennedsen et al., "Inside the Family Firm: The Role of Families in Succession Decisions and Performance," *Quarterly Journal of Economics* 122, no. 2 (2007): 647–691.

## Chapter 38

1. Morten T. Hansen, Herminia Ibarra, and Urs Peyer, "100: The Best-Performing CEOs in the World," *Harvard Business Review,* January–February 2013, http://hbr.org/2013/01/the-best-performing-ceos-in-the-world.

2. Jim Collins, *How the Mighty Fall and Why Some Companies Never Give In* (New York: HarperCollins Publishers Inc., 2009), 58–64.

3. Boris Groysberg and Deborah Bell, "Who's Really Responsible for P&G's Succession Problems?" *HBR Blog Network,* June 3, 2013, http://blogs.hbr.org/2013/06/whos-really-responsible-for-pg/.

4. This finding is reported in James S. Ang and Gregory Leo Nagel, "The Financial Outcome of Hiring a CEO from Outside the Firm," March 14, 2011, available at SSRN: http://ssrn.com/abstract=1657027. Private communications with Greg Nagel confirm that the finding still holds, although it is not reported in the most recent analyses of inside- and outside-hired CEOs.

## Chapter 39

1. Jeffrey A. Sonnenfeld, "What Makes Great Boards Great," *Harvard Business Review,* September 2002, http://hbr.org/2002/09/what-makes-great-boards-great/ar/1.

2. Chris Thomas, David Kidd, and Claudio Fernández-Aráoz, "Are You Underutilizing Your Board?" *MIT Sloan Management Review* 48, no. 2 (Winter 2007).

3. Jim Aisner, "Working Up With Boards—Jay Lorsch," *HBS Working Knowledge,* July 9, 2013, http://hbswk.hbs.edu/item/7298.html.

4. Claudia Pici-Morris and German Herrera, *Gender Diversity on Boards: Breaking the Impasse,* Egon Zehnder International, 2012, http://www.egonzehnder.com/leadership-insights/diversity-and-inclusion/gender-diversity-on-boards-breaking-the-impasse.html.

# Chapter 40

1.  Ashish Nanda and Kelley Morrell, *Strategic Review at Egon Zehnder International (A)*, Harvard Business School case study (Boston: Harvard Business Publishing, August 2004).

2.  Ranjay Gulati, Nitin Nohria, and Franz Wohlgezogen, "Roaring Out of Recession," *Harvard Business Review*, March 2010, http://hbr.org/2010/03/roaring-out-of-recession/ib.

3.  Per-Ola Karlsson and Gary L. Neilson, "CEO Succession 2008: Stability in the Storm," *Strategy + Business*, May 2009, http://www.strategy-business.com/article/09206?pg=all.

4.  Jean-Michel Caye et al., *Creating People Advantage in Times of Crisis How to Address HR Challenges in the Recession*, The Boston Consulting Group and European Association for People Management, March 23, 2009, https://www.bcg.com/documents/file15224.pdf.

5.  Warren G. Bennis and Robert J. Thomas, "Crucibles of Leadership," *Harvard Business Review*, September 2002, http://hbr.org/2002/09/crucibles-of-leadership/.

# Chapter 41

1.  Christoph Lueneburger, *A Culture of Purpose* (San Francisco: Jossey-Bass, 2014).

2.  Christoph Lueneburger and Daniel Goleman, "The Change Leadership Sustainability Demands," *MIT Sloan Management Review* (Summer 2010), http://sloanreview.mit.edu/article/the-change-leadership-sustainability-demands/.

# Chapter 42

1.  Marco Iacoboni, *Mirroring People* (New York: Farrar, Straus and Giroux, 2008), 248–254.

2.  Gautam Mukunda, *Indispensable: When Leaders Really Matter* (Boston: Harvard Business Review Press, 2012), 248–254.

# Chapter 43

1.  "List of Countries by GDP (PPP) per Capita," *Wikipedia*, http://en.wikipedia.org/wiki/List_of_countries_by_GDP_(PPP)_per_capita.

2.  Boon Siong Neo and Geraldine Chen, *Dynamic Governance: Embedding Culture, Capabilities and Change in Singapore* (Singapore: World Scientific Publishing Co. Pte. Ltd., 2007), 161.

3. Chua Mui Hoong, *Pioneers Once More: The Singapore Public Service 1959–2009* (Singapore: Straits Times Press Pte. Ltd., 2010).

4. Neo and Chen, *Dynamic Governance,* vii–viii.

5. Claudio Fernández-Aráoz, "In Search of the New Public Leader," *Ethos* 7 (January 2010): 69–73.

## Chapter 44

1. Claudio Fernández-Aráoz, "How to Pick the Next Pope," *HBR Blog Network,* February 13, 2013.

2. Chris Lowney, *Heroic Leadership* (Chicago: Loyola Press, 2003).

3. Jim Collins, *Good to Great and the Social Sectors: Why Business Thinking Is Not the Answer* (a monograph to accompany *Good to Great,* published by the author; Boulder, CO, July 24, 2005).

## Conclusion

1. Lucy Kellaway, "The Business Case for Hiring the Fat and the Ugly," *Financial Times,* April 28, 2013, http://www.ft.com/intl/cms/s/0/409d91ae-ac1a-11e2-9e7f-00144feabdc0.html#axzz2hRFKDTky.

2. David C. McClelland, "Testing for Competence Rather Than for 'Intelligence,'" *American Psychologist* (January 1973).

# Acknowledgments

Of course, getting this book written was not about the how or the what but the who.

Over the past three decades, I have been honored to work with clients who trust me to advise them on their most delicate and sensitive people issues, as well as on their own career and development decisions. I am deeply thankful for the opportunities and the associated learning.

I'm also grateful to the executive candidates who shared with me their glories, their disappointments, and their dreams; their unique life lessons have both inspired and humbled me. And I am thankful to the many political, religious, academic, and corporate leaders I've met who have further illuminated the challenges and opportunities of trying to surround oneself with the best and then help them thrive.

Our firm's founding chairman, Egon Zehnder, continues to inspire me like no one else, even long after his "retirement." With unprecedented levels of integrity and determination, he redefined the ethical and professional standards of the executive search profession. The publication of this book coincides with our firm's fiftieth anniversary; it is my gift to Egon, with the hope that it will inspire us toward the next fifty years of deep client impact and continuing greatness.

John Grumbar, board member and former chairman and CEO of Egon Zehnder, provided me with an incredible level of support and encouragement to follow my passion and write this new book.

Our current chairman, Damien O'Brien, my great friend of almost three decades, has also continued to be an invaluable source of guidance for my writing and speaking, just as he was an exceptional companion in our efforts to improve our practice and profession for so many years.

Dan Meiland, Egon's first successor, was the first person who encouraged me to publish in *Harvard Business Review* and become a professional speaker.

Rajeev Vasudeva, our great CEO, has been a wonderful colleague at our executive committee, and a true source of inspiration regarding the unique challenges and opportunities of family businesses.

Several of my colleagues at Egon Zehnder have played a very special role in the development of this book, and I'd like to thank them individually: Kentaro Aramaki, Tommaso Arenare, Mark Byford, Edilson Camara, Luis Cubillos, George Davis, Manuel de Miranda, Michel Deschapelles, Michael Ensser, Yoonmi Eom, Sanjay Gupta, Germán Herrera, Philippe Hertig, Martha Josephson, David Kidd, Eugene Kim, Simon Kim, Dennis Ku, Magnus Lambsdorff, Andrew Lowenthal, Christoph Lueneburger, Laurence Monnery, Anne-Claire Monod, Justus O'Brien, Jackie O'Sullivan, Claudia Picci Morris, Mike Portland, Verena Renze-Westendorf, Andrew Roscoe, Johannes Schmettow, Evelyne Sevin, Katrin Sier, Edwin Smelt, Ashley Stephenson, Karena Strella, Yan Sun, Lena Triantogiannis, Hideaki Tsukuda, Neil Waters, Elaine Yew, and Catherine Zhu.

Many other current or former colleagues at Egon Zehnder have also directly or indirectly contributed to this book, with invaluable insights and examples. The list includes Henrik Aagaard, Jill Ader, Jane Allen, Thomas Allgäuer, Gabriel Andrade, Joao Aquino, Raymond Bassoulet, Stephen Benkö, Fritz Boyens, Russell Boyle, Reinier Brakema, Horst Bröcker, Francesco Buquicchio, Emanuela Cancogni, Nick Chia, Peggy Cornwell, Alessandro Di Fusco, Carl Edenhammar, Chris Figgis, Angel Gallinal, Luis Garreaud, Ignacio Gasset, Nicola Gavazzi, Andrew Gilchrist, Luis Giolo, Andreas Gräf, Marcelo Grimoldi, Joe Haim, Thomas Hammer, Philipp Harmer, Dave Harris, Frank Heckner, Bill Henderson, Alan Hilliker, Mark Hönig, YL Huang, Fred Jacobsen,

Ru Jordaan, Rudolf Jordaan, Martha Josephson, Friedrich Kuhn, Selena LaCroix, Brigitte Lammers, Isabelle Langlois-Loris, André Le Comte, Kai Lindholdst, Victor Loewenstein, Tom Long, Brent Magnuson, David Majtlis, Ian Maurice, Rafaella Mazzoli, Yoshi Obata, Sikko Onnes, Fiona Packman, Christopher Patrick, Angela Pegas, Christopher Pfeiffer, Henny Purnamawati, Antonio Purón, Brian Reinken, Hélène Reltgen, Jörg Ritter, Robin Roberts, Celeste Rodgers, Riccardo Rossini, Norbert Sack, Pablo Sagnier, Isao Sakai, Gabriel Sánchez Zinny, Greig Schneider, Torgny Segerberg, Edmund Siah, Carol Singleton-Slade, Maitée Soares de Camargo, Raimund Steiner, Jorge Steverlynck, Jan Stewart, Ashley Summerfield, Ricardo Sunderland, Lily Surya, Hiroaki Takeda, Chris Thomas, Juan Torras, Kim Van Der Zon, Juan van Peborgh, Philip Vivian, Johannes Wardhana, Neil Waters, Andreas Zehnder, and Peter Zehnder.

Jim Collins deserves a very special mention for his extraordinary research and practice, which has so clearly validated the "first who" principle. It is always a pleasure to discuss leadership issues with Jim, and a privilege to be one of the critical readers of his unpublished work.

My writing companions on some of my HBR articles, Nitin Nohria, dean of Harvard Business School, and HBS professor Boris Groysberg (one of the best teachers I've ever seen in action) have been an extraordinary source of challenge, learning, and fun while we advance our knowledge of recruiting and development practices. Several other faculty members at HBS have also greatly advanced my understanding of these topics and have been very generous in meeting with me to discuss ideas and share their knowledge. They include Rakesh Khurana, Noam Wasserman, Rob Kaplan, and Ashish Nanda, now director of the Indian Institute of Management, Ahmedabad.

While working for McKinsey & Company in Europe many years ago, I learned firsthand that the right type of job rotation was the most effective way to grow and learn as an adult. Rolando Polli,

Marcial Campos, and Paco Moreno played a unique role at that critical stage of my early development.

Daniel Goleman continues to be an amazing inspiration for his past research on the relevance of emotional and social competencies, for his current work on attention as the most essential leadership skill, and for his extraordinary passion to make our world a better place. He has also been a key source of guidance and encouragement for me in my work as a writer.

I am also indebted to several members of Dan's Consortium for Research on Emotional Intelligence in Organizations, including its cochair, Cary Cherniss, as well as Richard Boyatzis, Lyle Spencer, Robert Caplan, Kathy Kram, Ruth Malloy, Rick Price, and Fabio Sala.

It has been a pleasure to discuss with Gregory L. Nagel, of Middle Tennessee State University, his original and promising research on CEO succession. I admire his academic work as much as his passion to improve the practice of people decisions where they matter the most.

Several colleagues and professionals have helped me understand how Singapore became one of the most competitive nations on earth by putting the best people into top political and public positions. My special gratitude and admiration go to my very dear friend Soo Hoon Lim, an extraordinary example of values and leadership.

Many extraordinary women have helped me conclude that the greatest opportunity for talent is not a place but a gender. Although the list is long, I would like to highlight Alessia Mosca in Italy, Hixonia Nyasulu in South Africa, Su-Mei Thompson in Hong Kong, and Sheryl Sandberg and Indra Nooyi in the United States.

Mayree Clark is an extraordinary member of that same league, and her initiative to launch Eachwin Capital, a firm that invests in publicly traded equities of companies with superior management teams and boards of directors, will surely demonstrate that superior investment returns depend not on the how (strategy), or the what (sector), but the who.

Jack and Suzy Welch also deserve a special mention for their incredible passion for surrounding themselves with the best, as well as for their generous efforts to give back and pass on their unique message globally, through the Jack Welch Management Institute and in countless other ways.

I want to thank Jeff Bezos's amazing leadership team at Amazon for their interest in my work, and particularly Sebastian Gunningham, Jeff Wilke, Tony Galbato, Ee Lyn Khoo, and Susan Harker. Getting to know these people confirmed to me that a high bar in recruitment and hiring decisions is the key to Amazon's extraordinary success.

My special gratitude goes to Roger Agnelli for sharing with me the story of his life and his amazing, people-focused leadership throughout his tenure as CEO of Vale.

My literary agent Helen Rees once again believed in me as an author and has shared my passion for this new book from the very first minute. She has become a unique partner and very dear friend.

Alison Beard at HBR has not only been an invaluable professional partner for me in developing this book, but my decision to write it actually hinged on her involvement. She is an exceptional professional and human being, and I decided to work with her on this book even before preparing a proposal. This proved to be one of my best people decisions ever. Alison's editing was as brilliant as her strategic advice, and working with her has been a unique pleasure.

I have been working with HBR since the late 1990s, and I have been amazed to witness the development of the extraordinary team and culture of this organization, particularly under the leadership of editor in chief Adi Ignatius. Tim Sullivan, editorial director of Harvard Business Review Press, has also been a wonderful professional partner, and I am thrilled each time I interact with the many participants in this project, including Kevin Evers, Stephani Finks, Jen Waring, Monica Jainschigg, Erin Brown, Mary Dolan, Tracy Williams, Nina Nocciolino, Ania Wieckowski, Ed Domina, Greg Mroczek, Allison Ryder, Dave DiIulio, Elie Honien, Vanessa Boris, Erica Truxler, and Adam Buchholz.

My assistant Joanna Eden, with whom I have had the pleasure to work for almost three decades, has once again exceeded even her own incredible standards of excellence and commitment, while making this process so easy and so much fun.

I have of course left the most important "who" for last. My beloved wife María is the love of my life and the greatest blessing I have ever received. She contributed directly to this book in so many ways, including her constant encouragement and support, her wonderful insights, and her infinite patience and understanding of my crazy levels of work and travel throughout the past year. In addition to being a brilliant professional and artist, she is an exceptional mother of the three wonderful children with whom God has blessed us. María and our delightful Ignacio, Inés, and Lucía constantly remind me, every single minute, that happiness in all the realms of one's life is not about the how or the what but the who.

# Index

# About the Author

CLAUDIO FERNÁNDEZ-ARÁOZ is a top global expert on talent and leadership and has been repeatedly ranked by *BusinessWeek* as one of the most influential executive search consultants in the world.

He is a senior adviser at the leading executive search firm Egon Zehnder and has been a member of its global executive committee for more than ten years. He founded the firm's management appraisal practice and served as global leader of its professional development, people processes, and intellectual capital development.

He is a frequent keynote speaker at business gatherings in the Americas, Europe, and Asia, as well as at leading management schools. His personal advice has been sought by the CEOs of major global companies, as well as by many progressive governments.

Fernández-Aráoz is the author of *Great People Decisions* (Wiley, 2007), a frequent contributor to *Harvard Business Review*, and a regular lecturer at Harvard Business School.

Born in Buenos Aires, Fernández-Aráoz graduated with a Masters in Science in Industrial Engineering from the Argentine Catholic University (Gold Medal, highest GPA ever at that school) and obtained his MBA at Stanford University (graduating also with honors as an Arjay Miller Scholar).

Before joining Egon Zehnder in 1986, he worked at McKinsey & Co. in Europe.

He is married to María, and is the father of Ignacio, Inés, and Lucía.